WORLD CLASS QUALITY

WORLD CLASS QUALITY

USING DESIGN OF EXPERIMENTS TO MAKE IT HAPPEN

Foreword by
Dorian
Shainin

Keki R. Bhote

American Management Association

Library of Congress Cataloging-in-Publication Data

Bhote, Keki R., 1925–
    World class quality : using design of experiments to make it
happen / Keki R. Bhote.
        p. cm.
    Includes index.
    ISBN 0-8144-5053-9
    1. Quality control—Statistical methods. 2. Process control—
Statistical methods. 3. Experimental design. I. Title.
TS156.B563   1991
658.5'62—dc20   91-19269
                                                          CIP

Printing number

10 9 8 7 6 5 4 3 2 1

To **Dorian Shainin**—an American icon and the world's foremost quality problem solver

and

To my son, **Adi K. Bhote,** whose practice of the Design of Experiments is beginning to exceed mine. It is a fond father's greatest reward.

Contents

Foreword

If you want a product to perform in the real world, you've got to consider everyday variables in its design, development, and manufacture. That lesson was never taught to me while at college. It was, however, my first instruction when I arrived at Hamilton Standard in 1936, twenty-two years old and fresh out of MIT.

"Forget what you learned in those textbooks," Tom Rhines, the senior engineer, advised. "Textbooks aren't the real world. The information we use comes from years of empirical testing."

In 1936, I learned that some information needed to make a product both right and reliable wasn't in the textbooks. It was in the parts. And, like a detective, I've been uncovering clues about how to design and manufacture quality parts ever since.

I had never planned a career in the then nascent field of quality control. When World War II began, I found myself helping Nash-Kelvinator, Frigidaire, and Remington-Rand—manufacturers of cars, refrigerators, and office machines—make propellers for B-17s. I was Ham Standard's licensee coordinator, and it was my job to ensure that these companies produced propellers as well as Ham Standard did. Production problems were inevitable. And since I was the guy from Ham Standard, engineers and operators looked to me for solutions. Solutions I didn't have. But clues, I would learn, abounded.

The folks at Nash-Kelvinator were confounded by steel

bolts that stretched and broke when tightened to the required torque. This didn't happen with just two or three bolts. All twelve barrel bolts on each of a dozen propellers had snapped. "You guys at Hamilton Standard have some crazy specs that don't work," the foreman said, greeting my arrival at the Lansing, Mich., plant where production had stalled. I tried torquing a bolt myself. Sure enough, it popped.

Manufactured by a local Michigan supplier, the steel bolts met our Rockwell C hardness specifications. The wrenches were applying the correct torque, but we went out and bought new wrenches, anyway. The bolts still snapped. We then tried tightening two bolts manufactured by a Hamilton Standard vendor in Connecticut, leftovers from our Kelvinator training sessions. They worked.

There has to be an obvious answer, I thought that evening in my hotel room, and I was bent on finding it. I focused on the bolts' 13 threads per inch and the load transmitted by rotation to tensile load. I developed some calculations which proved that more load was being applied than the steel could bear. And I surmised that poor finish on the Connecticut-made bolts was creating enough friction to absorb the extra load and prevent their fracture at our Hamilton Standard plant.

The next morning we assessed the finish of the threads under a magnifying glass. I was wrong. Our Connecticut bolts had a finer finish than those supplied to Kelvinator. But our concentration on the threads prompted us to consider something else—the corrosion-resistant cadmium plating. Was its lubricating characteristic making a difference?

So, we chemically removed the cadmium from one of the Ham Standard bolts. When tightened, the bare bolt held fast. A stripped Kelvinator bolt worked, too! Next, we swapped platings. The Ham Standard bolt with the Michigan plating broke. Kelvinator bolts sent east for plating in Connecticut didn't break. The parts talked—friction was a factor. The locally plated cadmium was acting as too much of a lubricant and didn't absorb the extra load. Our process-of-elimination approach was shared with Kelvinator's skeptical plating contractor. Startled by its simple logic, they went back to their factory and reduced the plating's lubricity.

That experience was my first real use of empirical analysis. I was surprised by its effectiveness and struck by the realization that if I didn't have the Hamilton Standard bolt for comparison, we never would have succeeded. Seemingly alike items, I learned, often have differences from which clues may be derived. And I gleaned that to generate clues, like any good detective, one cannot assume that the information provided is correct. You must confirm it yourself.

More than 50 years later, 24 statistical engineering techniques currently make up the Shainin System for Quality and Reliability Improvement. Each method has its own purpose. Depending upon one's goals, a Shainin strategy may include some or all of the techniques.

I didn't conceive all of these practices by myself. Some were built upon methodologies or concepts developed by such quality control and statistical luminaries as Leonard Seder, Warren Purcell, Sir Ronald Fisher, John Tukey, and Walter Shewhart. Others may never have been devised if it hadn't been for a timely observation by engineers with whom I worked.

Len Seder developed one of the practices, Multi-Vari, while at the Gillette Safety Razor Company in Massachusetts. Relatively unknown to most quality control people, Multi-Vari discovers assignable causes of variation, as well as many causes that conventional SPC classifies as random, and therefore, undiscoverable. It analyzes independent components of total variation in dimension, hardness, strength—any characteristic—while the item is produced repeatedly. Joe Juran tells me he had a hand in Multi-Vari, too. He suggested that Len take variation and chart it just like newspapers list trading activities on the New York Stock Exchange. Variation is divided into families, the largest of which leads to the source of the problem.

So effective is Multi-Vari, I've been utilizing it since the day Len asked that I give it a try. Later, Len wrote a paper for ASQC about Multi-Vari and maybe a few hundred people read it. Probably a handful figured it made enough sense to try it. The rest, too hesitant to break from traditional approaches, just added the paper to their stack of journals.

The late 1940s was an exciting time for the founding members of the New England ASQC sections. Len Seder, Joe Juran, Warren Purcell of Brown Paper Company, and I were trying to push quality control to new heights. Soon, Joe was teaching a ten-week course at New York University, spreading the gospel of quality control management. I became one of his guest lecturers.

Thanks to Joe's *Quality Control Handbook,* Precontrol is probably the best known of the Shainin system's statistical engineering techniques. It was developed during one of my first assignments at Rath & Strong, a Boston-based management consulting firm which I had joined in 1952.

Jones & Lamson, makers of optical comparators, had many job shop customers with lots too small to obtain $\overline{X}$ and R control limits. The company asked if $\overline{X}$ and R could be modified to work with smaller lots. Having worked with some 400 $\overline{X}$ and R charts at Hamilton Standard, I was very aware that statistical error increased as the sample size was reduced. Still, I felt optimistic that we could come up with an alternative. Jones & Lamson hired four of us at Rath & Strong for three solid weeks of work. Warren Purcell, Frank Satterthwaite, Bill Carter, and I hit the jackpot. We devised Precontrol in two-and-a-half weeks. Jones & Lamson received a half-week's refund.

We began with the recognition that all real process distributions have a higher probability of product in the center rather than in the tails, but their shapes are not the same. And we had to be able to work with a variety of distributions. Frank, an extraordinary Ph.D. statistician, picked a number of logical distributions. And he conducted statistical optimization studies to determine guidelines that could prevent an operator from making bad parts, or at least keep the number of bad parts to a minimum.

Sure enough, we found we could sense unsafe conditions, resulting from changes in the shape, width, and position of the process distribution, by counting two consecutive items in the outer regions of the tolerance. Frank calculated that to get optimum results, each warning or yellow zone had to be approximately one quarter of the tolerance. That left about half for the green center zone. Some statisticians who learn a little bit about precontrol scoff at its statistical rigorousness. *Fifty percent?* They can't believe that a number so well rounded could be statistically valid. It is. We've done Monte Carlo analyses to determine it.

We tried the technique on Jones & Lamson's grinding machines and the operators and engineers were amazed by the results. Management was so pleased, it flew me off to Endicott, N.Y., to sell precontrol to IBM, one of its key customers. Shorty Barrett, IBM's quality control manager, saw the logic in precontrol. With its simple traffic light–like color chart, precontrol appeals to operators by providing early warning of imminent trouble based on acceptable work. They don't have to make calculations; they just have to remember that red means stop, two consecutive yellows mean adjust, and green means go. Quick action, rather than entering data, does the job.

Precontrol wasn't a blessing for everyone at "Big Blue." Some operators couldn't get their machines to pass the set-up rule. Shorty had tried unsuccessfully to convince the tooling people to rebuild the machinery. Now, precontrol wouldn't let the machinery run until they did. Afterward, operators using precontrol produced good parts with little problem.

When I started at Rath & Strong, the only powerful quality approaches with which I had to work were Lot Plot, Multi-Vari, and Warren Purcell's assessment of classical Analysis of Variance. (I was getting by, albeit with some frustration, using sampling plans, Pareto analysis, and $\overline{X}$ and R charts.) Soon, precontrol was added to the roster. And I was eager to solve more tough quality and reliability problems, and if called upon, to develop a few more techniques along the way.

In the 1960s, the United States embarked on the ambitious effort of "landing a man on the moon and returning him safely to earth." From manufacturers of plastics and fabrics to cameras and computers, companies around the country vied for the opportunity to be a part of the space program. It was good PR and it was profitable.

Grumman, a manufacturer on Long Island, had carved out a niche making fighter aircraft for the Navy. Now, it wanted to build the craft which would land men on the moon and return them to the lunar-orbiting command service module. NASA specified that its lunar excursion module or LEM, as it was called, was to have an unparalleled margin of safety. The probability of the LEM failing to return the two Apollo astronauts to the command module could be no more than 5 in 10,000.

NASA would give primary consideration to the manufacturer which could best demonstrate 0.9995 reliability. Multiple Environment Overstress Probe Testing^SM, a technique I began developing at Ham Standard, had dramatically improved the reliability of hollow-steel propeller blades. To win the NASA contract, Grumman would put its faith in forcing failures, too.

I spent considerable time teaching overstress probe testing to Grumman's design and manufacturing engineers. And Grumman convinced NASA that with 90 percent certainty it could fulfill 0.9995 reliability without unreasonable cost and time.

Seven years later, the near-catastrophic flight of Apollo 13 would push the envelope of the LEM's reliability. En route to the moon, an oxygen tank exploded, crippling the command module's life support and fuel systems. The three astronauts entrusted their lives to the lunar module, which was made for two. The LEM shared its oxygen with the roomier command module, and rocketed the mated spacecrafts around the moon and back to the earth. Like many around the world, my heart was aflutter until the crew safely splashed down in the Pacific.

Motorola, winner of the first Malcolm Baldrige National Quality Award, began using the Shainin system in 1980, after a period when Motorola saw its market share being nibbled by overseas competitors. Carlton Braun, manager of Motorola's Seguin, Texas, plant, had heard of my approach and asked if I could conduct a seminar there. Keki Bhote was head of quality for Motorola's Automotive and Industrial Electronics

Division, of which Seguin was a part. He joined Carlton in the classes and got very excited about the techniques. Their engineers quickly employed them and solved some nagging quality problems.

Soon, Keki and I were bound for other Motorola plants where I taught more classes. Keki was a real champion for the Shainin techniques at Motorola. And as he moved up the ladder to senior corporate consultant for quality and productivity improvement, he spread the gospel of Shainin and empirical testing.

The results were remarkable. For example, using a few Shainin techniques—Multi-Vari, Variable Search Patterns[SM], and precontrol—one Motorola unit discovered the sources of imperfection in its semi-conductor manufacturing process. Once corrected, the operation produced 2.1 million semi-conductor chips without a single defect! Keki has been coaching and consulting Motorola's plants, its suppliers, and its customers all over the globe, with hundreds of Shainin experiments each year. Overall, Motorola has improved quality five hundred times in ten years. In the three years from 1988 to 1990, Motorola's cost of poor quality was reduced by nearly $1 billion. By 1992, it expects to reach its ambitious 6 sigma goal—no more than three to four defects per million.

Enthused by Motorola's successes, even before the Baldrige Award, Keki had been after me to write a book about my techniques. Each and every time, I begged off. "I'm just too busy with clients," I'd say. Finally, Keki asked if he could write a book about all that we had done together at Motorola. I agreed. It's been revised here to include many improvements my son Pete and I have made to those Shainin techniques covered by Keki.

I'm also grateful that Keki has stepped up on the soapbox to proclaim that you need not look to Japan for strategies to solve your quality and reliability problems. Just take a walk into your plant and talk to the parts.

With empirical testing, you'll find you can unravel the few controlling, yet often mysterious, variables in your materials, processes, and products—regardless of the industry involved. In time, like thousands of engineers trained in the Shainin techniques, you'll be a variation detective, too.

Dorian Shainin
Manchester, Conn.

Service Marks

The following names are service marks of Shainin Consultants, Inc.:

Attribute Search Patterns
B vs. C
Barrier B vs. C
Black Dot
Component Search
    Patterns
Delta Plot
Experience Plot
Isoplot
Isoplot Quickcheck
Multi-spec Search
Multiple B vs. C
Operations Search
    Patterns

Overstress Probe Test
Paired Comparisons
Pale Pink X
Pink X
Random Multi-spec Search
Randomized Sequencing
Rank Order Anova
Red X
Resistance Limit Transform
Shainin System
Source Isolation Squares
Tolerance Parallelogram
Variable Search Patterns
Visual Scoring Transform

PART I
Introduction

1

The Need for Simple, Powerful Problem-Solving Tools

The Killing of the Locusts: Brute Force

At the height of Mao Zedong's cultural revolution in China, the fields of one Chinese village were being attacked by swarms and swarms of locusts. Seeing their crops decimated, the villagers turned to Mao's little red book for guidance on how to get rid of this plague. They searched in vain. Nothing the great helmsman wrote seemed to fit until they came upon a piece of sound advice. Mao wrote that in the absence of any directive, people should devise their own solutions! That inspired the villagers to round up all able-bodied people and dispatch them to the fields to kill the locusts by hand, one by one. For seven days, hundreds of them labored long and hard until all the locusts lay dead. Had the same problem arisen in the United States, a few bags of insecticides would have done the job in one hour!

The Need: 90 Percent of U.S. Industry Does Not Know How to Solve Chronic Quality Problems!

The U.S. approach to solving chronic quality problems is similar to the brute-force efforts of the Chinese villagers. It

3

lacks the proper tools to do the job. Some may argue that the tools do exist, for example, statistical process control (SPC), Pareto charts, and cause and effect diagrams. These are weak tools, however, kindergarten tools, adequate for solving the simplest of quality problems but totally incapable of solving chronic quality problems that have festered weeks, months, or years at a time. In fact, over 90 percent of American industries do not know how to solve chronic quality problems! There is an urgent need, therefore, to prove to U.S. companies that simpler, but powerful, tools have been developed to solve and even prevent these chronic quality problems.

Objectives: Simple but Powerful Problem-Solving Tools

The purpose of this text is to:

1. Describe in simple, nonmathematical terms a variety of easy but statistically powerful techniques for solving any deep-seated quality problem that has resisted solution by traditional means. These techniques have been pioneered by Dorian Shainin, one of the quality gurus of the United States and one of the world's foremost quality problem solvers.
2. Coach *all* levels in a company—from engineers and technicians to line workers, from managers to customer and supplier companies—in the use of these eminently practical tools.
3. Progress from the current unacceptably high defect levels, such as 1 percent, to parts per million (ppm); from ppm to parts per billion (ppb); from ppb to zero defects; and, ultimately, from zero defects toward zero variation.
4. Prove that statistical process control (SPC) is not a problem-solving tool but only a maintenance tool and that within the world of SPC, control charts that are widely used in the United States are outdated, cum-

bersome, and statistically weak. Instead, precontrol is explained as a viable alternative to control charts. It is simple, cost-effective, and statistically far more powerful than control charts.

A Bonanza of Benefits

The very real benefits to those implementing these techniques, attested to by over 1 million practitioners in North America and the continents of Europe, Asia, and Australia, are:

1. Elimination of high scrap and rework, and on to zero defects and 100 percent yields
2. Drastic reduction of inspection and test, which are nonvalue-added activities
3. Enhanced customer satisfaction, because increased field reliability is a function of reduced plant defects
4. Extension of these techniques from problem solving in production to problem prevention at the design stage of the product and at the design stage of the process
5. Increased machine up time and machine yields to achieve the new minimum factory overall efficiency (FOE) of 85 percent*
6. Significant reductions in manufacturing cycle time through elimination of the dreary cycle of inspection, test, repair, reinspection, retest, re-repair, on and on
7. Significant reductions in design cycle time by designing the product right the first time and minimizing engineering changes after the start of production
8. Steep reductions in manufacturing cost through

---

*The discipline of total productive maintenance (TPM) requires that:
Factory Overall Efficiency (FOE) = % Up Time × % Yield × % Machine Efficiency (defined as optimum run time/[actual run time + setup time]) should be a minimum of 85 percent to be considered world class quality.

sharp reduction of the cost of poor quality, which typically runs from 10 to 25 percent of sales

9. Improved employee morale because success breeds success, instead of the festering of unsolved chronic problems by using traditional, ineffective problem-solving tools and the resulting "give-up-itis"

10. Extension of these techniques to suppliers to generate material quality, cost, and cycle time improvements and to customers to generate partnership and goodwill

11. Ability to leapfrog the Japanese in the use of powerful quality tools

12. Bottom line improvements: improved profitability, return on investments, and market share

Methodology: Road Map for This Book

Following the Introduction, which describes the need, objectives, and benefits of the book, Part I details the four stages of quality, from a primitive Stage 1 to a world class quality Stage 4, in ten areas of a corporation: management, organization, systems/measurement, tools, customers, design, suppliers, processes/production, support services, and people. It outlines the disciplines necessary to propel a company from lower stages on to a benchmark Stage 4. The remainder of the book focuses on tools as the area that is weakest in the United States' quest for quality leadership.

Part II is the most important feature of this book. It highlights the design of experiments (DOE), the principal weapon to go even beyond zero defects toward target values and zero variation. It starts by defining C_p and C_{pk} to measure variation, which is the antithesis of high quality. After briefly listing the statistical weaknesses of two better-known DOE techniques, the classical fraction factorial and the Taguchi orthogonal array, Part II concentrates on the Shainin techniques, specifically multi-vari charts, components search, paired comparisons, variables search, full factorials, B vs. C, and scatter plots. Each technique is explained in easy, nonmathematical, nonstatistical terms, along with case studies and practice exercises, in order to guide the reader in a user-friendly manner and enhance his implementation and success rate. In addition, Part II includes a comprehensive case study that uses six of the seven Shainin techniques, underlining their linkage, cohesiveness, and overall power.

Part III starts with a brief description of the elementary statistical problem-solving tools that are widely used in Japan but of little value in solving chronic quality problems. It then outlines the traditional statistical process control (SPC) tool, the control chart, highlighting its statistical weakness and other drawbacks. Then, it describes the newer SPC tool of precontrol, which is much simpler, more cost-effective, and statistically more powerful. In addition, it introduces two tools almost unknown to American industry, Positrol and process certification, both excellent techniques to keep important process variables and production quality peripherals under tight control. Further, the technique of operator certification is explained as the best way to prevent operator-controllable errors.

Part IV is a prescription for companies to ensure that the all-important work of DOE receives top management support and that its implementation becomes a way of life at all levels of a company.

Throughout this book, I quote figures and percentages regarding the state of American industry in the pursuit of quality. These do not result from single sources, but are based upon extensive discussions I have held with executives from a large number of companies.

Note about style: Women have been taking on a wider variety of and more influential roles in the business world. I welcome their presence. I still prefer, however, the use of the generic *he* to the various *he or she* alternatives. Throughout this book I have used *he* to refer to people of both genders.

2

The Four Stages of Quality

From Primitive Quality to World Class Quality

Before discussion of the methodology of design of experiments (DOE), the most powerful tool in solving chronic quality problems, it is necessary to establish the infrastructure of a comprehensive quality process that a company must construct in order to aspire to world class quality.

This chapter deals with four stages of quality, ranging from a primitive Stage 1 to a world class Stage 4. A company in Stage 1, called the stage of innocence, is in the Dark Ages of quality consciousness. A company in Stage 2, called the awakening stage, recognizes the importance of quality but is thrashing around without a firm game plan. A company in Stage 3, called the stage of commitment and implementation, is well under way on the road to world class quality. A company in Stage 4, called the world class stage, has become a benchmark company. It has entered the kingdom of quality heaven.

Table 2-1 is a matrix with the four stages of quality on one leg of the matrix and ten areas of a typical manufacturing company—management, organization, systems/measurement, tools, customer, design, supplier, process/manufacturing, support services, and people—on the other leg of the

Table 2-1. The four stages of quality.

Area	STAGE 1 Innocence	STAGE 2 Awakening	STAGE 3 Commitment/ Implementation	STAGE 4 World Class
1. Management	• Quality, a necessary evil • Problem detection/sorting	• Quality, a cost • Problem correction	• Quality, an economic imperative • Resources to prevention	• Quality, a superordinate value • Prevention—way of life
2. Organization	• Vertical Management • QC—the policeman	• Matrix • QA has quality responsibility, but little authority	• AD hoc problem-solving teams • Quality responsibility deployed to line functions	• Teams and focused factories • All employees responsible for quality
3. System/Measurement	• QC manuals • No quality costs	• QA policy/established • Quality costs gathered	• QA system established/ implemented/audited • Cost of poor quality reduced over 50%	• Continuous, never-ending improvement • Intangible quality costs attacked
4. Tools	• Data pollution, little analysis • No SPC	• 7 QC tools • Elementary SPC—control charts	• Design of experiments (DOE) • SPC: positrol, precontrol	• Design DOE • QFD, MEOST • Poka-Yoke, NOAC, TPM
5. Customer	• Profit over customer satisfaction • Selling vs. marketing • Voice of the engineer dominates	• Customer inputs sought • Customer measurements started	• Voice of the customer researched thru quality function deployment, conjoint analysis, etc.	• Customer enthusiasm • Next operation as "customer" pervades the organization
6. Design	• "Toss over the wall" to production • Concentration only on performance parameters • Reliability techniques unknown	• Eng./Mfg. teams for new products • FMEAs, FTAs	• Design for manufacturability • Accelerated life tests	• Design for zero variation and zero failures • Multiple environment overstress test • User-friendly built-in diagnostics
7. Supplier	• Adversarial relationships • Table-pound for price • AQLs: 1 to 2%	• Start of mutual trust and reduced supplier base • AQLs below 0.5%	• Partnership suppliers • 1 supplier per pt. no. • AQLs below 100 ppm	• Supplier an extension of company • Quality, cost, and cycle time help to suppliers • Self-certified suppliers
8. Process/Manufacturing	• High scrap, rework • Poor yields • Low uptime • C_{pk} unknown	• 80–90% yield • $C_{pk} < 1.0$	• Total defects/unit measurement • C_{pk} 1.33 to 2.0 • FOE concept introduced	• Scrap eliminated • Insp./test greatly reduced • $C_{pk} > 5.0$ • FOE > 85%
9. Support Services	• Poor quality, high cost, long cycle time • No measurements	• Next Operation as Customer (NOAC) concept introduced • Steering committee, process owners, and improvement teams established	• Internal customers measure internal supplier performance • Quality, cost, and cycle time improvement tools used	• Internal customer evaluation replaces boss evaluation • Financial incentives/ penalties established within NOAC
10. People	• People—pair of hands • Mgmt. overbearing • Pervasive fear • No training	• Quality circles • Mgmt. still not involved with people • Sporadic training	• Mgmt. participatory • Workers involved, multiskilled • Gain sharing • Training implemented on the job with measured results	• "Every employee a manager" • Workers empowered • Mgr. as consultant, not boss • From management to leadership

matrix. The following pages describe the four stages of quality for each area.

Management, the Bête Noire

Dr. W. Edwards Deming and Dr. Joseph M. Juran, two of the three American quality gurus (the third is Dorian Shainin), have long stressed that 85 percent of quality problems are the responsibility of management, only 15 percent the responsibility of the worker. In fact, Deming goes further. In his lectures, outlining his famous fourteen-point quality philosophy, he tells his management audiences that they are behind the times, almost stupid. And his listeners grin and bear it. There is no question but that everything, quality included, starts and ends with management.

In Stage 1, management looks upon quality as a necessary evil, a company's cross to bear. In Stage 2, it grudgingly admits that quality is important but that it costs money. It believes that high quality–low cost is an oxymoron.

In Stage 3, it finally recognizes that quality is not a negative—that it should not be dished out, by customers or to suppliers, in portions of fear and blackmail: "Embrace quality or you will lose our business; improve reliability lest the Damocles sword of product liability kill you; strengthen customer satisfaction lest the evil ghost of a Ralph Nader haunt you; worship quality lest the Japanese eat your lunch!" Stage 3 interprets quality not in these negative terms, but in the most glowing positive terms.

This reasoning is best illustrated by the famous PIMS (Profit Impact of Market Strategy) data, published by the Strategic Planning Institute. Based on over three thousand businesses, PIMS indicates that as quality goes from low to high, productivity, market share, profit on sales, and return on investment (ROI) also go from low to high by factors of 2:1 and more! In this remarkable correlation, quality is the cause, while these other business parameters that we tend to worship are only the effects. Quality is the input; the other parameters are only the outputs. Profits, ROI, and so on cannot be worked on. They are results. Quality can be worked on. Quality, therefore, in Stage 3 becomes an absolute economic imperative.

In Stage 4, management elevates quality to a superordinate value, among three of four values that a company holds sacred as part of its unchangeable beliefs. Among the one hundred or so truly progressive U.S. companies, management is in Stage 4, but the majority of companies still merit at best a Stage 2.

In another facet of management that addresses quality problems, Stage 1 is characterized by inspection and testing, sorting and screening—which are brute-force methods to achieve quality. Stage 2 develops corrective methods with problem-solving teams; Ford's 8-D (eight steps to diagnosis and correction) program is an example of a low-grade correction system. In Stage 3, management devotes its resources to problem prevention, along with support and follow-up of preventive disciplines, such as DOE. In Stage 4, prevention of quality problems becomes a way of life in product and process design, in manufacturing systems, and with suppliers. Even among the top one hundred progressive U.S. companies, quality problem resolution still languishes in a Stage 2 mainly because quality prevention tools are at best not addressed, at worst not known. Fifty percent and more of the remaining companies are mired in Stage 1, and the balance are crawling toward a Stage 1.5.

Organization: From Vertical to Horizontal Management

In the area of organization, Stage 1 employs the usual bureaucratic pattern, called vertical management, where communications tend to flow up and down, from and to the boss, rather than horizontally between departments. It promotes vertical silos, where high departmental walls tend to protect "turfs." In Stage 2, matrix management, under a product manager or project leader, tends to overcome the weaknesses of the Stage 1 functional organization, but on the other hand its structure, with a person having two "bosses," can be confusing and disruptive. In Stage 3, the team concept is introduced. Under the guidance of a top management quality steering committee, diagnostic, interdisciplinary teams are established to solve major quality problems. Finally, in Stage 4, the team concept, which never appears in a bureaucratic organization chart and which is, nevertheless, the most important advance in organizational development, becomes pervasive throughout the company and institutionalized within the framework of a focused factory. This pillar of cycle time management and Just-in-Time (JIT) encompasses producing, in an island within a behemoth factory, a narrow family of products for a narrow customer base with dedicated equipment and dedicated people, under the baton of a strategic business unit (SBU) manager.

The late Dr. Kaoru Ishikawa, the father of quality control in Japan, pointed to this fundamental flaw in American industry. He used the analogy of weaving. If there are only vertical threads, the cloth is going to be weak. It needs horizontal threads as well to strengthen the fabric. In a similar fashion, American industry, with its traditional vertical management, cannot hope to compete unless it reinforces its organizational fabric with horizontal management—with teams that cut across the vertical silos, just as customers and problems do. Except for the top U.S. companies that have achieved Stage 3, along with a sprinkling in Stage 4,* most American companies languish in Stage 1 or 2.

The place of the quality professional in an organization

---

*The latest advance in organizational development is the upside-down organization chart. On top is not the CEO, but the customer. Below him are the frontline troops within a company that come into frequent contact with customers. They need to be empowered and aided by all support services. They, in turn, must be supported by middle management. Finally, at the bottom of the organization chart is the CEO! He becomes the servant, not in a menial sense but in the biblical sense. He *serves* his people, not as a boss, but as a true leader, providing vision, inspiration. He is now the coach, the consultant, the teacher, the cheerleader. His main task is to *help* his people, technically or managerially or emotionally or spiritually!

also undergoes a fundamental transformation from stage to stage. In Stage 1, he reports at a low level, say, to the manufacturing manager. He is a policeman, a traffic cop, sorting and channeling rejects. In Stage 2, he is given the responsibility without the necessary authority. He is the proverbial messenger who gets shot at the first bad tidings. In Stage 3, responsibility for quality gets deployed to line functions—to engineering, manufacturing, and purchasing. In Stage 4, quality becomes so pervasive that all employees enthusiastically accept responsibility for quality in their own areas. (A simple test, during large town meetings within a company, is to ask, with a show of hands, how many people in the audience are responsible for quality. Very rarely do a forest of hands go up!) In Stage 3, the quality assurance department shrinks in size but is elevated in importance, typically reporting to a general manager of a division. In Stage 4, the quality assurance focal point is a one- to three-person entity reporting to the CEO. Such a person's role changes significantly from doer to quality consultant: a teacher and a coach, whose fundamental mission in life is not to blow the quality whistle but to help all employees accept their quality responsibility and reach their full quality potential.

With the exception of the top U.S. companies that have quality professionals in Stages 3 and 4, the largest percentage of the remainder are in Stage 2.

System/Measurement: "That Which Is Not Measured Is Not Managed"

Quality systems in Stage 1 are characterized by boiler-plate quality manuals that get periodically dusted off just before a customer's visit! These manuals regurgitate the same kindergarten directions about segregation of nonconforming material, calibration of equipment, and other fundamentals that progressive companies established decades ago. In Stage 2, the CEO establishes a quality policy, full of high-sounding rhetoric about the quality mission of the company. (The phenomenon of every company striving to have the best quality in its industry is reminiscent of 95 percent of fond parents in an affluent community asserting that their child is among the top 5 percent of the students in the class!) In Stage 3, a comprehensive quality system that goes far beyond a quality manual is established. It contains over seventy-five quality disciplines in various areas ranging from management to the worker, from design to the field. (Unfortunately, even quality professionals are not familiar with many of the most important and powerful disciplines.) This comprehensive quality system is then implemented throughout the organization and periodically audited, at least once a year. In Japan, such quality audits are conducted by top management and the board of directors; in the United States, if such audits are conducted at all, they are carried out by quality professionals who lack sufficient authority to force improvements. In Stage 4, the quality system ensures that there is continual, never-ending improvement at all levels of the company. Again, except for top companies, the great majority of U.S. companies are in Stage 2.

In the arena of measurement of quality progress, Stage 1 companies do not even know the importance of gathering, analyzing, and reducing quality costs. In its most basic aspects, the cost of poor quality includes warranty and customer returns, scrap and rework, analyzing, and inspections and tests. Typically, in U.S. companies, the cost of poor quality runs from 10 percent to 25 percent of the sales dollar. That is two to five times the profit on sales of an average U.S. company. To put it even more dramatically, through poor quality *each employee wastes, in companies that have not launched the cost of poor quality as a metric, from $100 to $200 per day!* If every U.S. company could reduce this shocking feature by no more than $30 per employee per day, this country could save $150 billion per year, which is enough to make a huge dent in our budget deficit and increase our GNP by at least 3 percent!

In Stage 2, quality costs are gathered and analyzed. In Stage 3, companies use the cost of poor quality as their quality

P&L statement, driving these costs ever downward. In Stage 4, companies include costs of poor quality not picked up by traditional accounting systems. They include lost sales due to poor quality, equipment down time, supplier quality and delivery delinquencies, long manufacturing and design cycle times contributing to large product and people inventories, and white-collar errors and the poor quality of management (the largest single cause). If these costs are included, the estimate could reach an astronomical 50 percent of the sales dollar, almost $500 per employee per day!

Even among the best of U.S. companies, the cost of poor quality (that can be picked up by accounting) is rarely below 5 percent. In Japan, according to Dr. Kano, a leading quality guru there, the best companies have achieved levels of 0.15 percent! What is worse, 80 percent of American companies do not gather—in fact, most of them do not even know—the cost of poor quality. Another 15 percent do not use it as a quality driver. This is truly a sad commentary on the state of quality in the United States, despite the management slogans that loudly proclaim a dedication to quality.

Tools: Separating the Men From the Boys

Management/leadership, people/teams, and quality systems are all important in the march to quality. But we need to give our good people tools to do the job, simple but powerful tools that all levels within a company or within a supplier organization can use. Otherwise companies will merely spin their wheels, with no traction to achieve a quality breakthrough. The most important quality tools, which will become commonplace in the twenty-first century, are listed in Table 2-2.

Stage 1 is completely ignorant of any of these tools. There is a drive to gather data. There is so much data that it can be described as data pollution. Nobody does much with the data. Computers only accelerate data pollution at the speed of light. Even SPC (which, unfortunately, most American companies

Table 2-2.   Quality tools for the twenty-first century.

Quality Tool	Area of Application
1. Quality function deployment (QFD); conjoint analysis	Capturing the voice of the customer, not the voice of the engineer
2. Design of experiments (DOE)	Reducing quality defects from percentages to parts per million (ppm) to parts per billion (ppb) to zero defects toward zero variation in product process designs and in supplier materials
3. Multiple Environment Overstress Tests (MEOST)	Reducing field failures to virtually zero within a product life cycle
4. Poka-Yoke	Preventing operator-controllable defects
5. Next Operation as Customer (NOAC)	Improving quality, cost, and cycle time in service operations (white-collar work)
6. Total Productive Maintenance (TPM)	Improving yield percentages, up time percentages, and machine efficiency percentages to achieve a minimum of 85% as a product of these 3 percentages

equate with nothing more than control charts) is unknown. In Stage 2, elementary quality tools, such as the seven tools of quality control widely used by line workers in Japan, are introduced. These consist of Plan, Do, Check, Act (PDCA), Pareto charts, cause and effect diagrams, histograms, and so on. Control charts plaster the walls of production in the mistaken belief that they can exorcize the defect devil! In Stage 3, design of experiments (DOE) is used to solve chronic quality problems in production, followed by Positrol to control key process parameters and precontrol as the only effective maintenance tool. In Stage 4, DOE is moved upstream to *prevent* quality problems at the design stage of the product and at the design stage of the process. The other tools listed in Table 2-2 are also implemented in a frontal attack to solve all quality problems, from customer to supplier, from management to the line worker.

The statistics indicate that only 50 percent of U.S. companies have reached even Stage 2. They labor long with control charts and achieve little. Only 10 percent to 15 percent are in Stage 3 and unfortunately most are dabbling with the more difficult and less effective Taguchi methods for DOE. There is not a single company in Stage 4 that embraces *all* the tools of Table 2-2. In fact, Table 2-3 depicts the dismal awareness and even more dismal implementation of these major quality tools.

Customer: From Profit to Total Customer Satisfaction

Management gurus, such as Peter F. Drucker, have long argued that the main objective of a business is not profit but customer satisfaction. Yet Stage 1 companies continue to worship profit while paying lip service to the customer. In the process, they achieve neither adequate profit nor true customer satisfaction.

Table 2-3. The level of awareness and implementation of the six major quality tools.

Number of Quality Tools	Percentage of Companies Having	
	Awareness	Implementation
1	50%	20%
2	30%	10%
3	15%	5%
4	5%	1%
5	1%	0%
6	0%	0%

The emphasis is on selling/designing products with the voice of the engineer rather than with the voice of the customer and then shoving the products down the customer's throat. Stage 2 begins to seek customer inputs and attempts customer feedback in a tentative manner. Stage 3 uses sophisticated techniques to research customer requirements, such as value research, sensitivity analysis, multi-attribute evaluation, quality function deployment, and conjoint analysis. Stage 4 concentrates on fulfilling all aspects of customer satisfaction—not just quality and reliability, but others such as performance, features, ergonomics, delivery, and price— elevating the process from customer satisfaction to customer enthusiasm. Stage 4 also expands the very definition of who is a customer. The external customer will always remain the king. But the internal customer, the next operation in a chain of internal customer–internal supplier links, must at least be treated as a prince, if the external customer is to become ecstatic about the company and its products.

Over 60 percent of our companies are still in Stage 1, even though they may believe that they are customer-oriented. At the other end of the scale, only a handful of companies have attained the ultimate Stage 4.

Design: The Prime Competitive Factor in the Years A.D. 2000 and Beyond

There is a growing realization today that the company that can design a product faster than its rivals can and get it to the market first will enjoy a distinctive competitive advantage. This is true not only because the design cycle time is shorter but also because the quality is better, the cost is less, and the manpower is lower. Coming into vogue is the half-half-half-half syndrome: designing in half the time, with half the defects, at half the cost, and with half the manpower that older designs required.

In Stage 1, designing is business as usual. The engineer designs the product in an organizational cocoon. The half-baked product is then tossed over the wall, with the time bomb ticking, for production to catch and muddle through. In Stage 2, engineering and manufacturing work together from the start of design to ensure a smoother product launch. In Stage 3, an interdisciplinary team, consisting of not only engineering and manufacturing, but also quality, purchasing, sales/marketing, and finance, is formed for new product introduction. Finally, in Stage 4, the responsibilities of each team member are clearly defined, milestone charts established, design reviews conducted, and sign-off mechanisms created. A contract between management and the team is drawn up, where the team commits to the quality, cost, and cycle time goals required for the product, while management commits to the needed resources and organizational support.

In terms of techniques, Stage 1 concentrates mostly on performance parameters. Stage 2 introduces elementary reliability techniques, such as failure mode effects analysis (FMEA) and fault tree analysis (FTA). Stage 3 advances to accelerated life tests in reliability and develops systematic methods to design for manufacturability (DFM) along with quantitative scores. Stage 4 is the ultimate: in quality, with design of experiments; in reliability, with multiple environment overstress tests; and in serviceability, with user-friendly built-in diagnostics.

Over 80 percent of companies are mired in Stage 1, with even the most elementary reliability tools unknown. However, brightening the design horizon are a few companies that prove the viability of Stage 4 designs.

Suppliers: A Win-Win Partnership

Direct labor constitutes less than 5 percent of the sales dollar, while material purchased from suppliers accounts for over 50 percent of the sales dollar. Yet a myopic management spends 50 percent of its time and energies on production while management of the supplier base suffers from benign neglect. Supply management—the partnership between purchasing, supplier quality assurance, engineering, and a narrow base of partnership suppliers—is becoming a key corporate strategy.

In Stage 1 companies, however, the customer-supplier relationship is adversarial. There is a total absence of mutual trust. In Stage 2, outright confrontation gives way to cautious suspicion and the beginning of trust. The large, unmanageable supplier base is reduced to preferred suppliers. In Stage 3, the supplier base is further reduced to a few partnership suppliers, where there is only one supplier per part number and no more than single-digit numbers of suppliers for an entire commodity. In Stage 4, the partnership supplier becomes a virtual extension of the customer company, except for ownership. The key word is *help*—active, concrete help— to the supplier as the only effective way for a customer company to achieve its objectives of the best quality, lowest cost, and shortest lead time from its suppliers.

In terms of quality, Stage 1 is characterized by the obsolete acceptable quality levels (AQL) of 1 percent and more. In Stage 2, these defect levels are reduced to 0.1 percent AQLs (one thousand parts per million) and less. In Stage 3, they are further reduced to one hundred parts per million and less. Finally, in Stage 4 the supplier quality is so good and under such perfect statistical process control that the supplier is certified to ship parts without the necessity of any incoming inspection.

It is estimated that 60 percent and more of U.S. companies are still in Stage 1, with another 30 percent in Stage 2; only a handful of companies have had the vision to implement Stage 4.

Process/Manufacturing: Where the Rubber Meets the Road

In most companies, all the quality efforts are concentrated in manufacturing. Unfortunately, defects are accepted as God-given, and brute-force inspection and rework are the conventional ways to filter out these defects. Defect prevention and the systematic reduction and eventual elimination of variation are almost unheard of.

This phenomenon is especially true in Stage 1 companies, where high scrap, poor yields, and low equipment up time are the order of the day. C_p and C_{pk} (explained in detail in Chapter 3) are foreign concepts. In Stage 2, scrap is attacked, while yields and equipment up time are improved, but brute-force methods are still the order of the day. C_p and C_{pk} measurements are initiated but are, generally, less than 1.0. In Stage 3, the concept of total defects per unit (tdpu) is introduced. It involves adding up all the defects at every checkpoint throughout a long production line and dividing by the total number of units passed. C_p and C_{pk}s are targeted at a minimum of 1.33 and up to 2.0. Total productive maintenance (TPM) is begun. The TPM metric measures yield percentages, up-time percentages, and machine efficiency (theoretical run time divided by actual run time plus setup time) percentages. These three percentages are then multiplied together to calculate factory overall efficiency (FOE). In Stage 4, scrap and repair are virtually eliminated, inspection and test are drastically reduced, C_p and C_{pk}s of 5.0 and over are achieved, and FOEs of 85 percent and more are registered.

It is a tragedy that the United States, which had built its past reputation on its ability to manufacture products, has now fallen not only behind Japan, but almost behind the four tigers of Asia: Korea, Taiwan, Hong Kong, and Singapore. However, thanks to the quality revolution in the past ten years, over 50 percent of U.S. companies have crossed over from Stage 1 to Stage 2. But only 10 percent are in Stage 3, while Stage 4 is almost devoid of any company.

Support Services: A Quality Desert

It is stated that an activity that is not measured is not managed. It is small wonder, then, that support services, where measurement of performance is almost nonexistent, are among the most antediluvian in terms of quality progress.

Stage 1 is characterized by poor quality, high cost, and long cycle time. What is worse, there are no measurements that have been established to monitor these important parameters. And if management attempts to introduce measurements, a rearguard guerrilla action is started by the white-collar troops to obfuscate the results at best and to derail them at worst. Stage 2 is the beginning of quality-mindedness. Steering committees, process owners, and improvement teams are established to provide guidance and continuity to quality improvement, and the concept of the next operation as customer (NOAC) is introduced as the fundamental building block of quality in support services. In Stage 3, the internal customer measures the performance of the internal suppliers against agreed-upon requirements, and proven quality, cost, and cycle time improvement tools are effectively used by the interdisciplinary teams. In Stage 4, internal customer evaluation replaces boss evaluation as a far more effective method of performance appraisal, and financial incentives/penalties are established to sustain the NOAC discipline.

In the United States, and indeed the world over, 99 percent of companies are in Stage 1 when it comes to white-collar operations. Only a few pioneering companies have entered Stage 2, and Stages 3 and 4 are empty monuments and likely to remain so even in the 1990s.

People: Employees as Partners

The United States considers itself the world's greatest political democracy, and yet industrially it remains an autocracy. Top-down management is the order of the day, despite the rhetoric that "people are our most important asset."

In Stage 1, the line worker is still looked upon as a pair of hands. In such Stage 1 institutions, there should be a sign at the guard entrance: "Please check your brain here. It will not be needed inside!" Management is invisible to the worker.

Holed up in his ivory castle, the manager is overbearing, authoritarian, and contemptuous of his workers. In turn, the employees are cowed or sullen. And fear is so pervasive that ideas and suggestions are not volunteered. The employees withdraw into their shells, content to do the minimum that is expected of them. Training is nonexistent.

In Stage 2, enlightenment enters. The importance of the worker is recognized and the formation of quality circles or improvement teams is encouraged. Management, however, is still remote. There is no mingling with the people and if communications exist at all, managers are transmitters, not receivers, talking instead of listening. The output of the quality circles is mediocre because whatever little training exists is sporadic and unfocused. People are not given truly powerful tools to solve quality problems.

In Stage 3, management has made a 180-degree turn. Managers regularly visit the workers, mingle with them, listen to them, and support them. The workers respond in kind. The corrosive influence of fear is removed and the suggestion pipeline, formal or informal, gets filled. Gainsharing, where workers are financially rewarded for surpassing reach-out goals, is considered both fair and profitable to the company. Training is implemented on the job with measured results.

Finally, in Stage 4, there is vertical job enrichment where every worker becomes a manager in his area of operation. Employees are empowered to make decisions, to take risks. They become frontline troops interfacing with customers. Management's role changes drastically from boss to coach, and from manager to leader, providing vision and inspiration.

Despite the drumbeat of propaganda about the importance of people, well over 60 percent of companies are still in Stage 1, another 30 percent in Stage 2, less than 10 percent in Stage 3, and a mere sprinkling of progressive companies are in Stage 4.

These, then, are the four stages of quality in ten areas of industry. Table 2-1 can help determine what stage of quality a company is in for each of the ten areas. It is an excellent

PART II

The Design of Experiments (DOE): Key to the Magic Kingdom of Quality

3

The Measurement of Process Capability

Japanese vs. U.S. Quality: Contrasting Techniques

Before we delve into the subject of variation and how to measure and reduce it, a comparison of the relative progress achieved in quality between Japan and the United States is in order. Figure 3-1, an adaptation of a chart prepared by the automotive industry, depicts this comparison.

Following World War II, U.S. quality reigned supreme, but Japan achieved parity by the late 1960s and has widened the gap in its favor ever since (see Figure 3-1A). The contrast becomes even starker when three major techniques to achieve quality—the traditional approach, SPC, and the design of experiments (DOE)—are examined. Traditional quality control consists of ineffective methods such as brute-force inspection, management exhortation, delegation of quality responsibility to a detached quality control department, and even sampling plans. As seen in Figure 3-1B, Japan abandoned this kindergarten approach as early as the 1960s, whereas the United States persevered with such obsolete tools well into the early 1980s.

SPC in Japan, "Too Little and Too Late"

As a result of W. Edwards Deming, Joseph M. Juran, and other U.S. trainers, Japan launched SPC in the 1950s and

Figure 3-1.   The contribution of traditional, SPC, and DOE tools to quality progress.

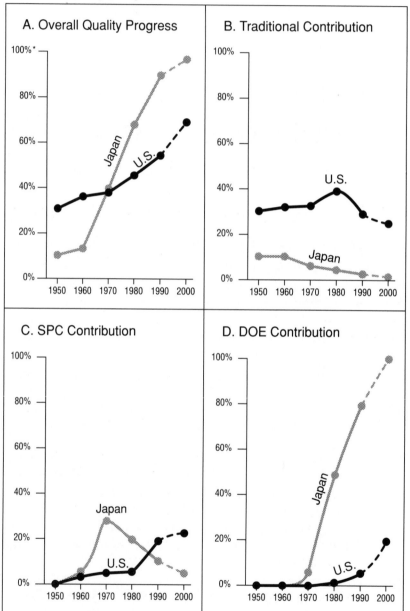

*100% Quality Progress = Zero Defects, Perfection

rode its crest till the early 1970s, when it concluded that SPC in production was too little and too late (see Figure 3-1C). Ironically, just as Japan was discarding SPC, especially for its professionals, the United States was rediscovering it. (SPC had been used in the United States during World War II, but the baby was thrown out with the bathwater when U.S. industry was on top of the industrial world and did not need fancy statistical tools.)

"If Japan Can, Why Can't We?"

What reushered in the SPC age in the United States was the airing of the NBC "White Paper" "If Japan Can, Why Can't We?" It gave the American public at large its first glimpse of the reasons behind Japan's success—quality in general and SPC in particular. Deming was rescued from the U.S. industrial wilderness and elevated as a prophet within his own country. Major companies scurried to jump on the SPC bandwagon. Unfortunately for the United States, SPC has become synonymous with control charts. As we shall see in Chapter 15, control charts are complex, costly, and almost useless in their ability to solve chronic quality problems.

Design of Experiments: Japan's Secret Weapon

The central thrust, and secret weapon, of Japanese quality is its widespread use of design of experiments (DOE). The object of DOE is to discover key variables in product and process design, to drastically reduce the variations they cause, and to open up the tolerances on the lesser variables so as to reduce costs. Figure 3-1D shows the spectacular rise in the use of DOE, especially since 1970. Hundreds of Japanese companies conduct thousands of these designed experiments each year to make product and process designs "more robust." They use the classical methods founded by Sir Ronald Fisher of Great Britain and, to a lesser extent, the orthogonal array developed by Genichi Taguchi of Japan.

In the United States, by contrast, DOE was unknown
until the 1980s, except to a small band of academics and
missionary statisticians and to the chemical/pharmaceutical
industries. But a belated movement is now under way. Mes-
merized by the Taguchi name, some American businesses
have been attracted to his methods. Their irrational logo is "If
it is Japanese, it must be good!" However, as we shall see
later, the Taguchi method is complicated, expensive, time-
consuming, and, above all, statistically flawed if interactions
exist.

From the U.S. point of view, there is a bad news–good
news aspect to DOE. The bad news is that the Japanese are
ten to twenty years ahead in the practice of DOE. The good
news is that the Shainin techniques, which are largely unknown in Japan, are simpler, cost-effective, and much more
statistically powerful. One of the objectives of this book is to
so coach American industry that it will be able to leapfrog
the Japanese in DOE, the centerpiece of quality tools.

"Variation Is Evil"

In cycle time management, it is often said that inventory
is evil—that inventory is the graveyard of poor management.
Similarly, in quality control, variation is evil and large variation is the graveyard of poor-quality management. Why is
this so? Why has the brand-new discipline of variation reduction become in a few short years one of the most important
tasks of the development engineer, manufacturing engineer,
and quality professional?

Customers Want Product Uniformity, "Like Peas in a Pod"

There are two reasons why variation reduction is so
important. First is the economic loss occasioned by customer
dissatisfaction. In the United States, there is a goalpost men-

tality concerning specifications. In football, the ball could pass very close to one or the other of the goalposts when a field goal is kicked. But as long as it is between the two goalposts, the kicking team scores the full field-goal points. We have the same view of specifications. A product can be barely within a specification limit. Yet we assume that the customer is satisfied 100 percent. And if the product is barely outside the specification limit, we assume that his satisfaction drops to zero. Figure 3-2A portrays this view. In actual practice, there is nothing so digital about customer satisfaction (assuming, to begin with, that the specification limits are right). Figure 3-2B portrays a more realistic, Japanese view,

Figure 3-2. The need for variation reduction.

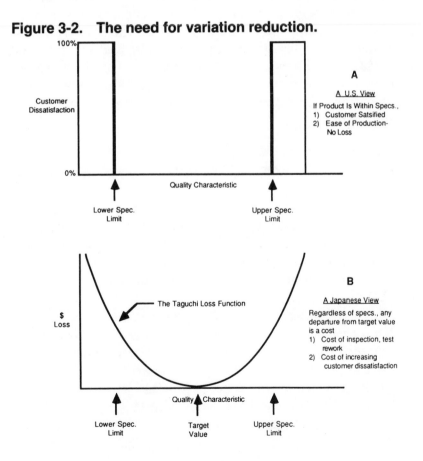

that customer dissatisfaction is at zero when a product parameter is at, or very close to, a target value or desired design center, and that it increases exponentially as the parameter moves away from the target value toward one end or the other of the specification limit. Loss of customer satisfaction can be measured in monetary terms. In fact, Genichi Taguchi of Japan has developed a loss function, a quadratic equation, to approximate this loss. Customers want uniformity of product, consistency, not units that vary all over the map, even if they fall within specification. This consistency is a feature of Japanese products that is seldom recognized by American manufacturers. An example is a comparison made by Ford of its own automatic transmission versus Mazda's. It found that the designs were essentially the same, and specifications were by and large the same. So were the parts. Yet the Ford transmission was noisier, less smooth, less reliable, and shorter-lived than Mazda's. The main reason was that the Ford parts varied widely, from part to part, even though they were within specifications. The Mazda parts were much closer to their design centers.

The Uselessness of Scrap, Repair, Inspection, and Test

A second reason why variation is evil is the enormous economic loss caused by poor quality (see the section on system/measurement in the four stages of quality in Chapter 2). It consumes 10 to 25 percent of the sales dollar. In down-to-earth terms, poor quality wastes $100 to $200 per employee per day.

The only surefire method to eliminate this waste is to so design a product and its process that the parameter is brought close to the target value or design center. There is no other way to get 100 percent yields the first time around or to achieve zero defects. Once this is done, production becomes a breeze, and manufacturing can then throw things together without the necessity of inspection and test, which add no value whatsoever.

Introduction to Process Capability: Cp

Before the variation in a parameter can be reduced, however, it must be measured. Two yardsticks, Cp and Cp$_k$, have become standard terminologies in recent years. Process capability, Cp, is defined as specification width (*S*) divided by process width (*P*). It is a measure of spread. Figure 3-3 depicts six frequency distributions comparing the specification width (always 40 − 20 = 20) to the process width.

Figure 3-3. Cp, a measure of variation.

(Upper Spec. Limit = 40; Lower Spec. Limit = 20; Process Width Defined As Range)

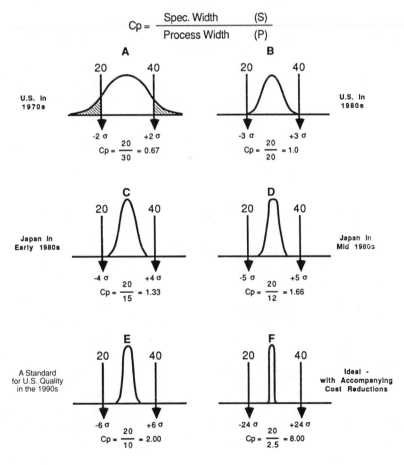

1. Process A in Figure 3-3 has a process width of 30 (as defined by range) to give a Cp of 0.67. It is a process that is out of control, with 2½ percent reject tails at both ends. This used to be the norm for U.S. processes before the SPC age of the 1980s. Today there are at least 30 percent of U.S. processes that are at or below this stage. They compensate for such an out-of-control condition by brute-force sorting, scrap, and re-work.

2. Process B has the process width equal to the specification width to give a Cp of 1.0. Although somewhat better than process A, it too can be considered almost out of control because it still has a reject tail of 0.13 percent, or 1,300 parts per million (ppm), at each end. At least 60 percent of U.S. processes have not advanced beyond a Cp of 1.0. The U.S. automotive industry has barely exceeded a Cp of 1.0. It has spent billions of dollars on statistical process control (SPC). Its savings are in the millions of dollars. That represents a return on investment of 0.1 percent in ten years! One can almost do better in a failed S&L bank! So much for our much-vaunted SPC and its principal instrument of control charts.

3. Process C has a Cp of 1.33, showing a margin of safety between the tighter process limits and the specification limits. The Japanese used a Cp of 1.33 as a standard for their important parameters in the early 1980s.

4. Process D, with a Cp of 1.66, is better, with an even wider safety margin.

5. Process E, with a Cp of 2.0, is an important milestone in the march toward variation reduction. Here the process width is only half the specification width. Some of the more progressive companies in the United States, including the author's, have established a Cp of 2.0 as a minimum standard for their own as well as for their suppliers' important quality characteristics. Several companies today are following Motorola's lead in striving for six sigma as a mark of quality excellence. Sigma (σ) is the standard deviation of a process, a measure of spread. Process E, with a Cp of 2.0, is the correct meaning of $\pm$ 6 σ; process D is at $\pm$ 5 σ; process C is at $\pm$ 4 σ; process B is at $\pm$ 3 σ; and process A is at $\pm$ 2 σ.

6. Process F, with a Cp of 8.0 (or ± 24 σ), is not only much better; it is also attainable and at a lower overall cost!

In fact, there is no limit to higher and higher Cps, of 10, 15, and more, so long as no recurring costs are added to the product or process and only the cost of design of experiments is incurred. These experimental costs should be looked upon as an investment rather than as a cost, in the best tradition of quality cost prevention. *It has been this author's experience that not only are costs not added with higher Cps; they are actually reduced. The time it takes to go from Cps of 1.0 or less to Cps of 5.0 and more is not measured in years but in weeks, generally with no more than one, two, or three well-designed experiments!*

Cp$_k$, a Better Measure of Variation and Process Capability

Cp is used only as a simple introduction to the concept of process capability. It does not take into account any noncentering of the process relative to the specification limits of a parameter. Such noncentering reduces the margin of safety and therefore has a penalty imposed, called a *K* or correction factor. The formulas are:

$$Cp \quad = \quad S/P$$

$$K \quad = \quad \frac{D - \overline{X}}{S/2} \text{ or } \frac{\overline{X} - D}{S/2} \text{ (whichever makes } K \text{ positive)}$$

$$Cp_k \quad = \quad (1 - K)\, Cp$$

where:

S = specification width; P = process width (± 3 σ limits); D = design center (D need not be at the midpoint of the specification width); $\overline{X}$ = process average.

When the process average, $\overline{X}$, and the design center, D, or target value, coincide, K is reduced to zero, making Cp and Cpk equal. If, however, the process average is skewed toward one end or the other of a specification limit, away from the design center, D, the value of K increases, causing a decrease in Cpk relative to Cp.

This is illustrated in Figure 3-4. Figure 3-4A has a wide spread, with a Cp of 0.71. Because its design center, D, and its average, $\overline{X}$, coincide, the Cp and Cpk values are the same at 0.71. Figure 3-3B has a narrow spread, with a respectable Cp of 2.5. But because it is located close to the lower specification limit, the K factor penalizes it to give a poor Cpk of 1.0. Figure C has a broader spread than Figure B, with a lower Cp of 1.67. But it is closer to the design center, D, than is Figure B and so the K factor has less of a penalty, resulting in a Cpk of 1.33, better than that of Figure B. Figure D is ideal, with both a very narrow spread and a centered process, to give a Cp and Cpk of 5.0.

A simpler formula for Cpk, and one especially useful for a single-sided specification limit, is:

$$Cp_k = \frac{\overline{X} - \text{nearest specification limit}}{\text{½ process width}}$$

or

$$\frac{\text{nearest specification limit} - \overline{X}}{\text{½ process width}}$$

whichever makes Cpk positive.

Cpk is an excellent measure of variability and process capability because it takes into account both spread and noncentering. (In process control, centering a process is much easier than reducing spread. Centering requires only a simple adjustment, whereas spread reduction often requires the patient application of design of experiment techniques.) As in Cp, the objective should be to attain a higher and higher Cpk,

Figure 3-4. C_{pk}, a measure of process capability.

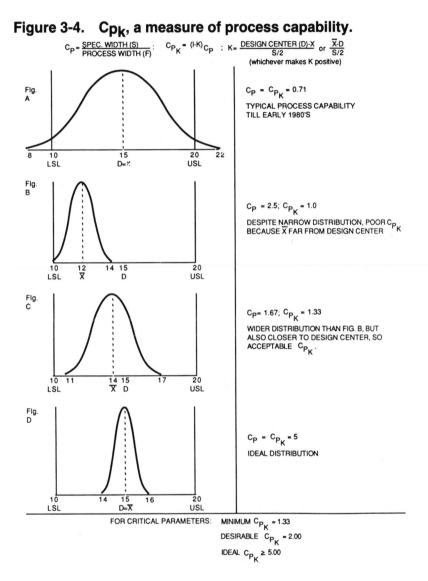

$$C_p = \frac{\text{SPEC. WIDTH (S)}}{\text{PROCESS WIDTH (F)}} \quad ; \quad C_{P_K} = (1\text{-}K)\,C_p \quad ; \quad K = \frac{\text{DESIGN CENTER (D)-X}}{S/2} \text{ or } \frac{\overline{X}\text{-D}}{S/2}$$
(whichever makes K positive)

Fig. A

$C_P = C_{P_K} = 0.71$

TYPICAL PROCESS CAPABILITY TILL EARLY 1980'S

Fig. B

$C_P = 2.5; \ C_{P_K} = 1.0$

DESPITE NARROW DISTRIBUTION, POOR C_{P_K} BECAUSE $\overline{X}$ FAR FROM DESIGN CENTER

Fig. C

$C_P = 1.67; \ C_{P_K} = 1.33$

WIDER DISTRIBUTION THAN FIG. B, BUT ALSO CLOSER TO DESIGN CENTER, SO ACCEPTABLE C_{P_K}.

Fig. D

$C_P = C_{P_K} = 5$

IDEAL DISTRIBUTION

FOR CRITICAL PARAMETERS: MINIMUM $C_{P_K} = 1.33$
DESIRABLE $C_{P_K} = 2.00$
IDEAL $C_{P_K} \geq 5.00$

with a C_{pk} of 2.0 considered merely as a passing milestone on the march past zero defects to near-zero variation. C_{pk} is also a convenient and effective method of specifying supplier quality, better than the old 1 percent and 2 percent acceptable quality levels (AQLs) or even the newer and lower defect levels expressed in parts per million (ppm).

Practice Exercise on Cp and Cpk: The Press Brake

A press brake is set up to produce a formed part to a dimension of 3″ ± 0.005″. A process capability study reveals that the process limits are at 3.002″ ± 0.006″, i.e., at a minimum of 2.996″ and a maximum of 3.008″. After corrective action, the process limits are brought under control to 3.001″ ± 0.002″.

Question 1. Calculate the C_p and C_{pk} of the old process.

Question 2. Calculate the C_p and C_{pk} of the corrected process.

These are the answers to the practice exercise on C_p and C_{pk}:

Question 1. Specification width (S) = 0.010″; process width (P) = 0.012″

So $C_p = S/P = 0.010/0.012 = 0.833$

$\overline{X} = 3.002″$; design center $(D) = 3.000″$

So $K = \dfrac{\overline{X} - D}{S/2} = \dfrac{3.002 - 3.000}{0.005} = \dfrac{0.002}{0.005} = 0.4$

Therefore $C_{pk} = (1 - K)C_p = (1 - 0.4)\,0.833 = 0.5$

Question 2. Specification width (S) = 0.010″; process width (P) = 0.004″

So $C_p = S/P = 0.010/0.004 = 2.5$

$\overline{X} = 3.001″$; Design Center $(D) = 3.000″$

So $K = \dfrac{\overline{X} - D}{S/2} = \dfrac{3.001 - 3.000}{0.005} = \dfrac{0.001}{0.005} = 0.2$

Therefore $C_{pk} = (1 - K)\,C_p = (1 - 0.2)\,2.5 = 2.0$

Using the simpler and alternate formula for C_{pk}:

$$\text{In Question 1: } Cp_k = \frac{3.005 - 3.002}{0.006} = \frac{0.003}{0.006} = 0.5$$

$$\text{In Question 2: } Cp_k = \frac{3.005 - 3.001}{0.002} = \frac{0.004}{0.002} = 2.0$$

4

Variation: An Industrial Epidemic

Measurement Does Not Equate With Improvement

Chapter 3 quantified variation with the introduction of C_p and C_{pk}. But measuring variation does nothing to reduce it. An analogy from the world of dieting is apropos. Thousands get up on their weighing scales each day to wage the battle of the bulge. If measurement alone could do the trick, Americans would be the thinnest people on earth! What is needed is an honest analysis of the causes of excess weight—eating habits, type of food, lack of exercise, etc.—before a disciplined regimen of weight reduction is begun. Similarly, the many causes of variation in industry should be analyzed before a systematic attack on variation is mounted. Variation is so widespread in industry that it can be likened to an epidemic. *The new quality mission, therefore, is to inoculate products and processes against variation.*

The Many Sources of Variation

This chapter will outline the many sources of variation, their underlying causes, and the general approaches to variation reduction. Table 4-1 presents a capsule summary. The

Table 4-1. Sources, causes, and reduction of variation.

Source	Causes of Variation	Variation Reduction
Poor Management	• No knowledge of or policy on variation reduction • No resources or time allocated to DOE • No championship or involvement in DOE • No DOE training or its implementation • SPC and control charts, especially for problem solving	• Top management training in DOE overview • Management steering committee for DOE • DOE training and workshops for tech. population • Monitoring the DOE "process" rather than just goals and results
Poor Product/Process Specs.	• Selling over marketing • Pushing state of art designs • Wide tolerances vs. target values • Reliability not a specification • No DOE in systems testing	• Value research and multi-attribute evaluation and quality function deployment • Evolutionary vs. revolution designs • Target values and DOE to achieve them • Optimizing old equipment, not junking it • Multiple environment overstress tests for reliability • Extension of DOE in customer application • Total productive maintenance
Poor Component Specs.	• Fascination with technology • Indiscriminate and tight tolerances • Boiler plate specs; supplier-published specs • Monte Carlo and worst case analysis • Formulas linking variables nonexistent, wrong, or unable to determine interaction effects	• DOE techniques at pilot run stage to separate important variables from unimportant ones • Realistic tolerance parallelogram (scatter) plots
Inadequate Quality System	• Comprehensive quality system not developed • Quality peripherals overlooked	• Infrastructure of a quality system • Positrol, process certification, precontrol
Poor Supplier Materials	• Too many suppliers • Control by negotiations and table pounding • AQL, incoming inspection	• "Best in class" partnership supplier • Physical proximity, continuous help • DOE training • Cp_k of 2.0 as a minimum
"Operator" Errors	• Poor instructions, training • Poor processes, materials, equipment • Design for nonmanufacturability • External inspection • "Pair of hands" syndrome	• Training in 7 QC tools and DOE • Encouragement, support, management involvement • Self-inspection and poka-yoke (foolproofing) • Gain sharing • Empowerment

major sources of variation can be grouped into six categories:
(1) poor management, (2) poor product/process specifications,
(3) poor component specifications, (4) inadequate quality system, (5) poor supplier materials, and (6) "operator" errors.

Poor Management

Deming and Juran assert that 85 percent of quality
problems are caused by management and only 15 percent by
workers on the line. They are being kind to management: The
split is actually closer to 95–5. Although there are many
dimensions to the quality problems caused by management,
its sins of omission and commission with respect to variation
include the following:

- Lack of knowledge about the impact of variation on
  overall quality and cost
- No coherent policy on variation reduction
- No resources or time allocated to the design of experiments (DOE), but unlimited quantities of both ex-
  pended on fire fighting
- No leadership in variation reduction in terms of goals,
  sponsorship, championship, or involvement
- No DOE training or no follow-up of training with implementation
- Equation of quality progress with SPC and control
  charts

How very different from an enlightened management
philosophy, as illustrated by an internal memo from William
Scollard, vice-president of engineering and manufacturing at
Ford: "Our new quality thinking should be reduced process
variability around the nominal as an operating philosophy for
never-ending quality improvement."

The attack on variability in management must begin
with an understanding of the economics of variation reduction. It requires a top management steering committee to
launch training in DOE, followed by workshops and "learning

by doing" for the technical people. The committee should also be involved in the DOE "process" for improvement and not just limit itself to formulating high-sounding goals and tracking results in sterile operation reviews.

Poor Product/Process Specifications

Most product specifications are either vague, arbitrary, or wrong. Occasionally an important quality characteristic requirement is missing, never having been even suspected. Process specifications are even worse!

A major cause of this variation lies in the difference between selling and marketing. In selling, management or the engineer determines product requirements in isolation and then forces the product down the throats of customers, through slick advertising and other high-pressure tactics. In marketing, the company first makes a painstaking effort to explore what the customer wants and then designs products to fit those needs. It is tragic that eighty years after Julius Rosenwald and Robert Wood laid the foundations of marketing and with it built Sears Roebuck into a giant merchandiser, most American companies still "sell" rather than "market" their products. The worst crime in this source of variation is to design and build products efficiently, even with zero defects, that the customer does not want!

"The voice of the engineer" must be replaced by the "voice of the customer." The latter is then translated into meaningful product specifications through use of tools such as quality function deployment (QFD), which is the most well-known. But there are also simpler and less costly techniques that are almost as effective. These include value research, multi-attribute evaluations, and conjoint analysis. This author is currently researching a process that embraces the best of these techniques at the least cost and lowest cycle time.

Other reasons for poor product/process specifications are:

- The engineer's ego in creating a "state of the art" design, with his name etched onto it in perpetuity

- Use of broad specification limits and tolerances rather than a focus on target values or design centers for product/process parameters
- Infrequent use of reliability in mean time between failures (MTBF) or mean time between assists (MTBA) as a specification
- Lack of systems testing in the customer's application with a design of experiments approach to identify important and interacting variables

The variation reduction antidotes are to:

- Use an evolutionary, rather than a revolutionary, approach to product/process design, one in which no more than a fourth of the design is changed at a given time
- Establish target values
- Save and optimize old processes through DOE, rather than junk them in favor of capital-intensive new equipment with its own host of problems
- Utilize multiple environment overstress tests as the most powerful tool in reducing product/process variations in reliability
- Extend design of experiments to field testing at the customer's site

Poor Component Specifications

Even assuming that product specifications have been optimized as shown above, there is another major pitfall, the inadequate conversion of product specifications into component specifications. The reasons are:

- Engineering's fascination with technology.
- Engineering's proclivity toward tight tolerances.
- Engineering's reliance on previous component drawings, "boiler plate" requirements, or supplier's published specifications.

• Reliance on the computer for determining components tolerances. This can only be done if the formula governing the relationship between the output (or dependent variable) and the independent component variables is known. In many complex designs, involving scores of independent variables, even an Einstein could not develop such a formula. This is a major weakness in many Monte Carlo simulation exercises.

• A "worst case" analysis and design with an extremely low probability of occurrence in actual practice. This is an appreciable addition to cost with no value added.

• No way of having knowledge of an unknown, synergistic interaction effect between or among component variables even when there is a mathematical formula for the relationships between variables.

All these excess variations can be overcome—at the prototype engineering pilot run, or production pilot run stage—by well-designed experiments, fully detailed in Part II, that can pinpoint the important variables, their ideal values (or levels), and their realistic tolerances.

Inadequate Quality System

Besides management, product, process, materials, and workmanship, there are many quality peripherals that can cause variation. Poor instructions, lack of environmental controls, lack of preventive maintenance, and test instrument variations are but a few examples. The control of these types of variation requires a comprehensive quality system, along with techniques such as Positrol and process certification. Chapter 16 is devoted to reining in these quality peripherals.

Poor Supplier Materials

Next to design, variations in supplier materials contribute the most to poor quality. The traditional approach of having multiple suppliers for the same part to assure quality, delivery, and cost is obsolete and counterproductive. So are negotiations, table pounding, and quality improvement by fiat and by remote control. So are AQL, sampling plans, and incoming inspection. The only way to improve supplier quality and to reduce variability is to:

- Demonstrate, first, that your own company is highly professional in the field of quality in general and in the design of experiments in particular
- Ascertain that the supplier is both committed to improvement and capable of entering into a long-term partnership with you
- Select a supplier who is in physical proximity to you and small enough and hungry enough to accept your professional coaching in DOE techniques
- Specify minimum C_{pk}s of 2.0 and more for important parameters, bypassing the useless milestones of AQLs, ppms, sampling plans, and postmortem incoming inspection

"Operator" Errors

Operator variations and inconsistencies are the causes of quality problems most frequently cited by orthodox management. Such citations, however, almost always reflect a general ignorance of quality—management at its quality worst. Worker defects are only the effects. The underlying causes are more likely to be:

- Poor instructions, goals, training, and supervision
- Poor processes, materials, test equipment
- Poor design for manufacturability
- Use of external inspection as a crutch
- Assumption that workers are but "pairs of hands," hired from the neck down

When these roadblocks to quality work are removed, workers—99 percent of whom are well-motivated to begin

with—will almost always come through with sterling performance. The steps to variation reduction in this area, in general terms, are encouragement, support, the elimination of fear, and management's mingling among and active involvement with the workers. Financial incentives for improved performance, such as gainsharing, should also be given serious consideration.

In specific terms, there should be a concerted move away from external inspection to neighbor inspection and, eventually, self-inspection, aided by *poka-yoke* (foolproof) methods, such as the use of automatic equipment and sensors to buttress visual checks. More important, workers can not only be trained in the seven tools of QC as practiced widely by Japanese line workers, they can also be trained in the even easier design of experiment tools described in Part II. It has been this author's experience that some of the most adventurous and rewarding DOE work has been conducted by line workers and technicians, once trained, more than by their more cautious and conservative engineering counterparts.

5

Three Approaches to DOE: Classical, Taguchi, and Shainin

Chapter 3 deals with the measurement of variation, introducing C_p and C_{pk} as parameters. Chapter 4 outlines the many causes of variation and lists general variation reduction techniques. Subsequent chapters concentrate on the most powerful of these techniques, generically called the design of experiments (DOE). They are particularly important in two areas: for resolving chronic quality problems in production, and at the design stage of both product and process. A chronic problem can be described as a product with an unacceptable defect rate, one that is measurable in higher dollar waste and that has defied traditional engineering solutions for a long time. (Some chronic problems have one, two, and three birthday candles on them!) It is especially important that DOE techniques be used on all *new designs* so that chronic quality problems in production can be *prevented* before fire fighting becomes necessary.

The *objectives* in both areas are as follows:

1. Identify the important causes or variables—whether they be product or process parameters, materials or components from suppliers, environmental or measuring equipment factors.

2. Determine the main effects and interaction effects of these important variables.
3. Reduce the variation on the important variables (including the tight control of interaction effects) through close tolerancing, redesign, supplier process improvement, etc.
4. Open up the tolerances on the unimportant variables to reduce costs substantially.

Classical vs. Taguchi vs. Shainin DOE

There are three approaches to the design of experiments: the classical, Taguchi, and Shainin. The classical approach is based on the pioneering work of Sir Ronald Fisher, who applied design of experiment techniques to the field of agriculture as early as the 1930s. It is difficult to conceive of an application in which there are as many variables—and as many interacting variables—as agriculture. In the United States, classical DOE has been extended to chemical processes. Beyond these disciplines, it had—until recently—remained in the province of academia. Its principal champions are Box and Hunter, two eminent professors and statistical authorities.

Dr. Genichi Taguchi of Japan adapted the classical approach to refashion the old technique of orthogonal arrays. While the Taguchi methods have not been universally accepted in Japan, some leading Japanese companies have adopted them. One of these, Nippon Denso, conducts over three thousand experiments each year, probably almost a third of the total DOE experiments of all kinds in the entire United States! In this country, AT&T and Ford have promoted Taguchi methods. As a result, several companies such as Xerox, I.T.T., United Technologies, and some Ford suppliers have started to use the orthogonal array approach, with marginal success.

The third DOE approach is a collection of techniques invented or perfected by Dorian Shainin, a consultant to more than eight hundred leading companies in the United States. Unfortunately for this country, Shainin's methods have not received the publicity they so richly deserve.

Table 5-1, under techniques, lists the principal methods used by each approach. The classical tools start with fraction factorials and end with evolutionary optimization (EVOP). The Taguchi methods use orthogonal arrays (inner and outer) in "tolerance design," employing analysis of variance and signal-to-noise for statistical evaluation. Each of the Shainin methods is detailed, chapter by chapter.

All three approaches are far superior to conventional SPC, which attempts to solve chronic problems by means of control charts—a total waste of time. All three approaches are also far superior to old-fashioned experiments, taught in universities and widely practiced by traditional engineers, in which one variable at a time is varied, with all other variables kept rigidly constant. Besides the inordinate amount of time needed for such experimentation, the central statistical weakness of this approach is the chronic inability to separate main from interaction effects. The results are frustration, the endless chasing of one's own tail, and high costs.

The Trouble With Taguchi

The greatest blessing that Taguchi has conferred on industry is that he has taken design of experiments out of the rarefied realm of university professors and statisticians and into the design laboratories and production floors of industry. His methods can be summed up in the motto "Don't just sit there, do something!"

Nevertheless, his orthogonal array approach has several fundamental flaws. To start with, it is complicated. A Taguchi course takes from three days to two weeks, leaving most participants lost! Engineers are uncomfortable with statistical concepts, such as analysis of variance, F tests, and signal-to-noise ratios. It is also expensive. With inner arrays multiplied by outer arrays, the number of experiments can reach several hundred.

Table 5-1. Three approaches to the design of experiments.

Characteristic	Classical	Taguchi	Shainin
Principal Techniques	• Fraction factorials • EVOP	• Orthogonal arrays	• Multi-vari, components search • Paired comparisons, variables search, full factorials, B vs. C • Scatter plots and other tools
Effectiveness	• Good in the absence of interactions (20% to 200% improvement) • Poor if interactions are present (small gains; retrogression possible) • Limited optimization	• Good in the absence of interactions (20% to 100% improvement) • Very poor if interactions are present (minimal gains; retrogression likely) • Very limited optimization	• Extremely powerful regardless of interactions (100% to 1000% improvement common, 10,000% improvement achievable) • Retrogression rare • Maximum optimization
Cost/Time	*Moderate* (8 to 50 experiments)	*Moderate,* if no interactions (8 to 36 experiments for inner array alone) • High if interactions present (several trials of same experiment; 64 to over 300 experiments for inner and outer arrays combined)	*Low* (3 to 30 experiments)
Complexity	*Moderate* • ANOVA required • 3 to 5 days of training	*High* • Inner and outer arrays multiplied • S/N and ANOVA required • 3 to 10 days of training	*Low* • Mathematics "embarrassingly" simple • 1 to 2 days of training
Statistical Validity	*Low* • Saturated designs, with confounding of main and interaction effects	*Poor* • Highly saturated designs, with extreme confounding of main and interaction effects • S/N only effective if ratio of mean to standard deviation is constant • The objective to make a design "robust" against noise factors is worthy, but the means to achieve this are poor. • Nonrandomization—a glaring flaw	*High* • Clear separation of main and all low and high order interactions
Versatility	*Low* • Only 2 tools available	*Poor* • Only one tool available	*High* • 7 tools available to tackle a wide range of problems
Scope	• Requires hardware • Main use in production	• Can be used at design stage if formula governing input and output variables is known • Main use in preproduction	*High* • Requires hardware • Can be used at prototype, preproduction, and production stages
Ease of Implementation	*Moderate* • Statistical knowledge and computers required • Engineers discouraged by complexity	*Poor* • Statistical knowledge and computers required • Engineers "turned off" by complexity and modest results	*High* • Minimal statistical knowledge required • Engineers, production, direct labor, and suppliers gravitate to its use, encouraged by excellent results.

Further, Taguchi's approach grudgingly accepts randomization only if it is convenient! This is a cardinal statistical sin, because variables not included in the experiments should be allowed equal opportunities of entering or leaving the experiments. Another weakness is that the Taguchi approach selects factors to be included in the experiment through brainstorming. This is a highly subjective technique that introduces too many variables and wastes time and money. (By contrast, the Shainin approach of homing in on the family of the important variables through techniques like the multi-vari and component search and paired comparisons greatly reduces the number of experiments required.)

Most important of all, the Taguchi approach does not consider interactions, unless, on the basis of engineering judgment, a severe interaction is "suspected." This is a grave structural flaw. One can seldom guess even the main variables that contribute to variation, let alone interactions among them.

The orthogonal array belongs in the family of fraction factorials and suffers from the same statistical weaknesses as does that generic family of saturated designs, namely the confounding of interaction effects (especially the higher-order interaction effects) with main effects.

In short, its results are suboptimal, with benefits that can and do evaporate.

Please refer to the Appendix of this book for a detailed statistical explanation of the weakness of all fraction factorial (classical) experiments in general and the Taguchi orthogonal array in particular. The Appendix is abstracted from a comprehensive paper, "Better Than Taguchi Orthogonal Tables," by Dorian and Peter Shainin, published in *Quality and Reliability Engineering International,* Vol. 4, 1988, pp. 143–149. It clearly states that the confounding with multiple aliases (i.e., false names) of interaction effects with main effects, caused by highly saturated experiment designs, makes the fraction factorial statistically weak and the Taguchi orthogonal array even weaker. The results, if interactions are present, are modest or transient gains.

In fact, many DOE practitioners, disenchanted with the

poor results of the Taguchi methods, are turning to the Shainin DOE system for a quality breakthrough.

The Shainin Diagnostic Tools

*Along with his pioneering contribution to reliability perfection through multiple environment overstress tests, Dorian Shainin has created DOE tools that can diagnose and greatly reduce variation, leading us beyond zero defects, beyond the milestone of C_{pk} of 2.0, to near-zero variability. These tools are:

- *Simple*—understood by engineers and line workers alike. The mathematics involved are unbelievably, almost embarrassingly, elementary!
- *Logical*—based on common sense.
- *Practical*—easy to implement in production, in design, with suppliers.
- *Universal in scope*—applicable in a wide range of industries, big and small, process-intensive as well as assembly-intensive.
- *Statistically powerful*—in terms of accuracy, with no violations of statistical principles.
- *Excellent in terms of results*—with quality gains not in the inconsequential range of 10–50 percent improvement but in the 100–1,000 percent range!

*Dorian Shainin is one of the "gurus" of quality on the American scene. Among the others, Phil Crosby is the showman, useful for companies in the Dark Ages of quality. Juran is superb for general quality management. Deming now concentrates on twisting top management's tail. Shainin alone is the consummate "tool" man, the master problem solver. Shainin is a portly man. But unlike the Aga Khan, who was weighed in gold and, later, in diamonds, Shainin is truly worth his weight in both gold and diamonds for his tremendous contribution to SPC and the design of experiments. Techniques like the lot plot plan, precontrol, multi-vari charts, components search, paired comparisons, and variables search were either invented by him or forged into sledgehammer power by his adaptations of earlier developments. This author is an unabashed disciple of Dorian Shainin and is deeply grateful to this great American for his tutelage.

Table 5-1 compares the classical versus Taguchi versus Shainin methods in terms of effectiveness, cost, complexity, statistical validity, applicability, and ease of implementation. It is obvious that the Shainin tools run circles around the other two in almost every characteristic. They can help the United States leapfrog the Japanese in their own game of concentration on design over production quality.

Variation Reduction: A Detective Journey to the Red X

Figure 5-1 represents a time-tested road map to variation reduction. It consists of seven DOE tools invented or perfected by Dorian Shainin. They are based on his philosophy: "Don't let the engineers do the guessing; let the parts do the talking." What he means is that the addition of DOE to the expert technical knowledge of the engineer is an unbeatable combination for solving any chronic quality problem. The analogy of a detective story is appropriate in this diagnostic journey, shown in Figure 5-1. Clues can be gathered with each DOE tool, each progressively more positive, until the number one culprit cause—the Red X in the Shainin lexicon—is captured, reduced, and controlled. The second most important cause is called the Pink X, the third most important the Pale Pink X. Generally, by the time the top one, two, or three causes—the Red X, Pink X, and Pale Pink X—are captured, well over 80 percent of the variation allowed within the specification limits is eliminated. *In short, a minimum C_{pk} of 5.0 is achieved—not in five years, not in four, three, two, or even one year, not even in months—but in weeks, with just one, two, or three DOE experiments!*

Table 5-2 presents a capsule summary of the seven DOE tools, their objectives, and where and when each is applicable. It gives a sample size, depicting the unbelievable economy of experimentation.

Figure 5-1.   Variation reduction: a road map.

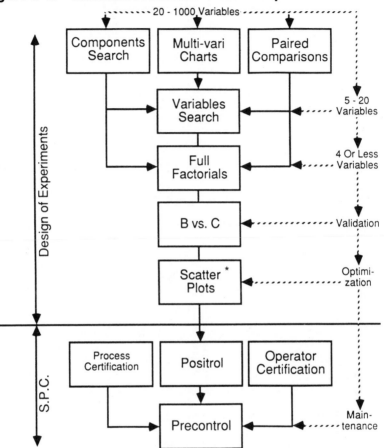

*The more appropriate (but lengthy) terminology for this technique is "realistic tolerance parallelogram plots."

SPC Tools: The Tail That Has Been Wagging the DOE Dog

It is only when the diagnostic journey, using the DOE tools depicted in Figure 5-1, has ended—with a substantial reduction in variation—that we can afford to descend from the highlands of DOE to the lowlands of SPC. The true role of SPC, therefore, is *maintenance* to ensure that variation, once

Table 5-2. The seven DOE tools.

Tool	Objective	Where Applicable	When Applicable	Sample Size
Multi-Vari Chart	• Reduces a large no. of unrelated, unmanageable causes to a family of smaller and related causes, such as time-to-time, part-to-part, within part, machine-to-machine, test position-to-test position, etc. • Detects nonrandom trends	• Determines how a product/process is running, a quick snapshot, without massive, historical data that are of very limited usefulness • Replaces process capability studies • In some white-collar applications	At engineering pilot run, production pilot run, or in production	Min. 9–15 or until 80% of historic variation is captured
Components Search	From hundreds or thousands of components/subassemblies, homes in on the Red X, capturing the magnitude of all important main effects and interaction effects	Where there are 2 differently performing assemblies (labeled "good" and "bad") with interchange-able components	At prototype, engineering pilot run, production pilot run, production, or field	2
Paired Comparisons	Provides clues to the Red X by determining a repetitive difference between pairs of differently performing products	Where there are matched sets of differently performing products (labeled "good" and "bad") that cannot be disassembled	Same as components search	4 to 8 pairs of "good" and "bad" product
Variables Search	1. Pinpoints Red X, Pink X, etc. 2. Captures the magnitude of all important main effects and interaction effects 3. Opens up tolerances of all unimportant variables to reduce cost	• Where there are 5 to 20 variables to investigate • Excellent problem-prevention tool	• Excellent in R&D, development engineering, and in production for product/process characterization • Also pinpointing Red X after multi-vari or paired comparisons	1 to 20
Full Factorials	Same as variables search	• Practical only where there are 2 to 4 variables	Same as variables search	1 to 20
B vs. C	• Validates superiority of a new or better (B) product process over a current (C) one with a desired statistical confidence (usually 95%) • Evaluates engineering changes • Reduces cost	• Follows one or more of the above 5 tools • When problem is easy to solve, B vs. C can bypass above tools • In some white-collar applications	• In prototype, pilot run, or production	Usually 3 Bs and 3 Cs
Realistic Tolerance Parallelogram (scatter plots)	Determines optimum values (levels) for Red X, Pink X variables and their maximum allowable tolerances	• Following above 6 tools	• In pilot run of product/process	30

captured and reduced, is incarcerated in a maximum security prison. These SPC tools, shown in Figure 5-1, will be discussed in detail in Part III.

Yet if a poll were taken in American industry among those companies that have attempted variation reduction, you would find that 90 percent started with SPC, a clear case of the SPC tail wagging the DOE dog. And 90 percent of *them* would equate SPC with little more than control charts!

6

Multi-Vari Charts: To Home In on the Red X

The main *purpose* of a multi-vari chart is to reduce a large number of unmanageable possible causes (or factors or variables; these are synonymous terms) of variation to a much smaller family of variables containing the Red X. This narrows the field of inquiry from, say, thirty to a hundred variables or more down to a more manageable number, for instance one to twenty. These prime suspects can then be further narrowed down to the Red X and Pink X with a variables search or full factorials. In several cases, the clues from a multi-vari chart are strong enough to directly pinpoint the Red X, precluding the need for further experiments.

Multi-Vari Chart Methodology

A multi-vari chart is a stratified experiment to determine whether the major variation pattern is positional, cyclical, or temporal (time-related). If the greatest variation is temporal, the several factors contributing to positional or cyclical variations can be eliminated or given a much lower priority for further investigation. Examples in each pattern of variation are:

Positional

- Variations within a single unit (e.g., porosity in a metal casting) or across a single unit with many parts (e.g., a printed circuit board with many components or a particular chip location within a wafer)
- Variations by location in a batch-loading process (e.g., cavity-to-cavity variations in a mold process)
- Variations from machine to machine, operator to operator, or plant to plant

Cyclical

- Variation between consecutive units drawn from a process
- Variation among groups of units
- Batch-to-batch variations
- Lot-to-lot variations

Temporal

- Variations from hour to hour, shift to shift, day to day, week to week, etc.

Figure 6-1 shows the three types of variation that are possible in a quality characteristic. A few units, generally three to five, are produced consecutively at any given time. Then some time is allowed to elapse before another three to five consecutive units are run off. The process is repeated a third time, and, if need be, a fourth or fifth time, *until at least 80 percent of the out-of-control variation in the process being investigated is captured.* This is an important rule in multi-vari exploration.

By plotting the results of the multi-vari run, you can determine if the largest variation is positional (within unit), as in variation A of Figure 6-1, or cyclical (unit to unit), as in B, or temporal (time to time) as in C. The multi-vari chart should never be confused with a control chart. It is a snapshot in time of how variation in a process is "breathing." One can call it a stethoscope of variation. For this reason, it is the only one of the DOE tools in which the running or checking sequence should not be randomized.

Multi-Vari Case Study: The Rotor Shaft

A manufacturer producing cylindrical rotor shafts with a diameter requirement of 0.0250″ ± 0.001″ was experiencing excessive scrap. A process capability study indicated a spread of 0.0025″ against the requirement of 0.002″, i.e., a C_{pk} of 0.8. The foreman was ready to junk the old turret lathe that produced the shaft and buy a new one for $70,000 that could hold a tolerance of ± 0.0008″, i.e., a C_{pk} of 1.25. However, on the advice of a consultant, the plant manager directed that a multi-vari study be conducted before the purchase of the new lathe, even though its payback period would be only nine months.

Figure 6-2 shows the results of the multi-vari chart. The four positional (within each shaft) variations describe taper changes from the left side of each shaft to the right, and out-of-round conditions, that is, maximum diameter and minimum diameter on each side of the shaft. The cyclical variations, from one shaft to the next, are shown by the thin connecting lines between the four readings of each shaft. The temporal variations, from one time period to the next, are also shown.

A quick glimpse reveals, even to a novice unfamiliar with multi-vari charts, that the greatest variation seems to be time to time, with the largest change occurring between 10 A.M. and 11 A.M. This provided the foreman with a strong clue. What generally happens around 10 A.M.? A coffee break! When the next sample of three shafts was taken at 11 A.M., the readings were very similar to those at the start of production at 8 A.M. He was now able to equate the time variations with temperature. As the day progressed, the readings got lower and lower, until there was a dramatic reversal about 10 A.M., brought on by the machine being shut down for the coffee break. Temperature, therefore, could be a possible Red

Figure 6-1.   Three types of possible variations in multi-vari charts.

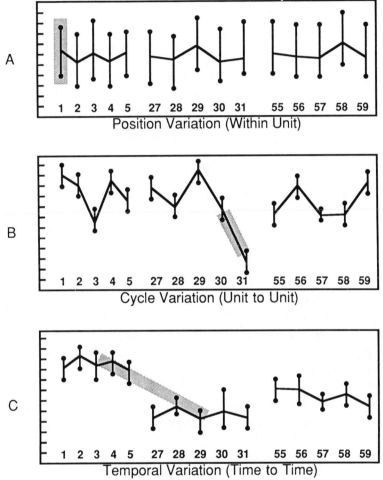

X. The foreman discovered, to his embarrassment, that the amount of coolant in the lathe tank was low. When the coolant was added to the prescribed level, the time-to-time variation, which accounted for approximately 50 percent of the allowed variation (specification width of 0.002"), was reduced to an inconsequential figure. With one stroke, adding coolant, almost 50 percent of the allowed variation was eliminated!

Figure 6-2.   The rotor shaft multi-vari chart.

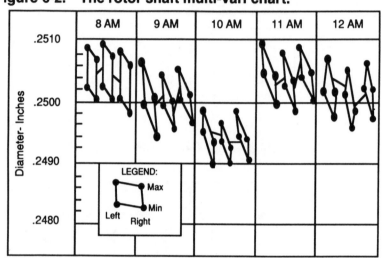

The foreman believed that the unit-to-unit variation, accounting for about 5 percent of the total allowed variation, was not worth investigating. However, the within-unit positional variation showed the second-largest variation—about 10 percent and 30 percent of the allowed variation, respectively, for the taper and out-of-round conditions.

The variation in taper showed a significant nonrandom pattern, with the left side always higher than the right side. (It is important that every multi-vari chart be scanned for such nonrandom trends.) This led the foreman to conclude that the cutting tool, as it traversed the rotor shaft from left to right, was not parallel to the axis of the shaft. A slight adjustment to the guide rail reduced taper to almost zero. Thus another 10 percent of the allowed variation was virtually eliminated.

Finally, the foreman attacked the cause of the out-of-round condition in each shaft. This was traced to a worn eccentric bearing guiding the chuck axis. New bearings were installed for a total cost of $200, including labor. This eliminated nearly 30 percent of the allowed variation.

Variation Type	% of Total Variation	Variation Cause	Variation Correction	% Variation Reduced
Time to time	50%	Low level of coolant	Coolant added	Nearly 50%
Within unit	10%	Non-parallel setting	Setting adjust-ment	Nearly 10%
Within unit	30%	Worn bearings	New bearings	Nearly 30%
Unit to unit	5%	?	—	—

In summary, the following results were achieved in the rotor shaft multi-vari study: The total variation in follow-on production was reduced from 0.0025″ down to 0.0004″ and the new C_{pk} was 0.002/0.0004 = 5.0. The benefits: zero scrap and a cost avoidance of $70,000 through retaining the old machine.

There is a moral in this story. Too often, American industry is prone to throw out an old machine or process before investigating the underlying causes of variation, which 90 percent of the time can be eliminated or reduced without the crushing burden of capital investment. The Japanese, on the other hand, painstakingly search out the causes of variation in the old machines and optimize yields. However, the techniques they use, for the most part, are brute-force methods, such as cause and effect diagrams, as compared with the elegant Shainin tools, of which the multi-vari is only one example.

Practice Exercise on Multi-Vari Charts

In a multi-vari study on the adhesion of tiles mounted on a strip, the data shown below are arranged (1) within each strip, (2) strip to strip, and (3) time to time. A plot of the data is also shown (H and L are the highest and lowest adhesions, respectively, within each strip; X is the average within each strip; O is the average of all three strips within each time interval.)

Multi-Vari Study: Tile Adhesion								
	8:30 A.M.			1 P.M.			3 P.M.	
Strip nos.	11	12	13	267	268	269	314	315	316
	66	59	54	60	57	47	38	14	56
	56	58	32	53	37	57	9	43	39
	58	66	59	44	46	48	54	8	60
	65	48	48	50	44	49	60	60	58
	67	63	72	58	52	56	57	38	60
Strip avg.	62.4	58.8	53.0	53.0	47.2	51.4	43.6	32.6	54.6
Time avg.		58.1			50.5			43.6	

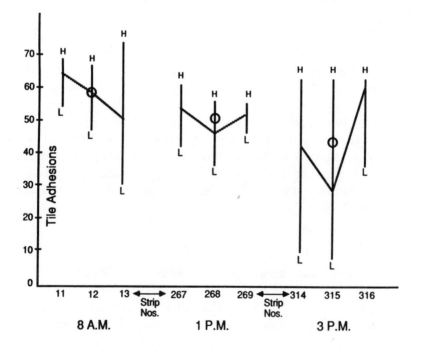

Question 1. Identify the three sources of variation and their contribution to the total variation.

Question 2. What nonrandom trends do you detect?

The answers to the two questions are:

Question 1. The within variation is 62 grams. The strip-to-strip variation is 35 grams. The time-to-time variation is 15 grams.

Question 2. With respect to nonrandom trends, (1) there seems to be a deterioration in adhesion with time; (2) the 3 P.M. adhesions show the greatest variation and the greatest deterioration; (3) the 1 P.M. adhesions have the least variation; (4) there is a fair degree of consistency among the highest adhesions within each strip, indicating that if the root cause of the variations is determined (with follow-on variables search or full factorial experiments), a respectable adhesion between 60 and 70 can be achieved; (5) the first two strips in each time period have about the same adhesion spread; the third strip is different from the first two; (6) the second strip is always slightly lower than the first; (7) tiles one and five appear to have higher adhesions than tiles two, three, and four.

7

Components Search: Easy, Surefire Clues

Components search is another simple but powerful technique whereby a very large number of possible causes of variation (even over one thousand) can be reduced to the family of the Red X or the Red X itself. Reduction to the lowest number of possible causes is the *objective*.

Principle, Prerequisites, and Procedure

A game analogy can be used to illustrate the *principle* behind components search. The game is to ask a person secretly to select any word in a large unabridged dictionary having about 2^{17} (132,072) words. The object is for the "problem solver" or questioner to locate the exact page containing the selected word through "yes" or "no" responses to the problem solver's questions. The questioner starts with the middle page number in the dictionary and asks if the word is located beyond the middle page. A "yes" or "no" answer eliminates half the pages of the dictionary. The next question of a similar nature eliminates three-fourths of the dictionary pages and so on, until, by the eleventh "yes" or "no" answer, the exact page location is determined. Within another six tries (a total of seventeen), the exact location of the word within the page—and hence the word itself—can be pinpointed.

A similar rapidly converging process of elimination is used in components search, where the culprit variable can be traced from an assembly of, say, over one thousand parts down to a subassembly of, say, one hundred parts, to a sub-subassembly of twenty parts, down eventually to the one or few Red X parts.

Components Search Principle

The uniquely novel features of components search have been misunderstood by some evaluators, who seem to consider it to be a form of fractional factorials. Nothing could be further from the truth. Fractional factorials, as explained in the Appendix, suffer from their inability to separate the true controlling cause of the observed variation from its "confounding aliases," i.e., interacting causes, many of which can be present. Moreover the Red X often turns out to be an interaction, rather than a single cause or variable.

Rather than merely confirming or denying a preselected set of causes, as is attempted in classical DOE, components search actually discovers and isolates unexpected controlling causes, be they main causes or higher-order interactions. And it achieves this isolation with much less total testing.

Understanding the distinctly different role of each of the four stages of components search will greatly help to correct mistaken evaluations. Table 7-1 lists each stage along with its objective.

Stage 1: ballpark stage. This stage determines if the Red X and Pink X are trapped or not among the components or factors to be investigated; i.e., are they in the ballpark? Stage 1 concludes this with a statistical confidence of 95 percent and thus enables the experimenter to proceed or not proceed to the next stage.

Table 7-1.   The four stages of components search.

Stage	Objective
1 Ballpark	To determine if Red X, Pink X are among the causes being considered. It also assures repeatability of the disassembly and reassembly process
2 Elimination	To eliminate all unimportant causes and their *associated interaction effects*
3 Capping Run	To verify that the important causes are truly important and that the unimportant causes are truly unimportant
4 Factorial Analysis	To quantify the magnitudes of the important main causes and their interaction effects

Stage 2: elimination stage. The purpose of Stage 2 is to eliminate not only all the unimportant main causes *but also the associated interaction effects associated with each unimportant cause.* It does this, as with the binary search principle in the dictionary game, by pairs of interchanged tests. With each interchange, a tremendous number of potential interacting causes and the main effect (the single factor or cause changed) are simultaneously "energized." Again, with 95 percent statistical confidence, at each test pair only the absence of a Red X eliminates that tremendous host of main causes and their associated interactions.

Stage 3: capping run stage. This stage verifies or validates that the important causes selected in Stage 2, when combined, continue to be important and that the unimportant causes identified in Stage 2 are unimportant.

Stage 4: factorial analysis. This stage is not another experiment but an analysis drawn from Stages 1 and 2 in a full factorial matrix to quantify the magnitudes of the important main causes and their interaction effects.

What are the *prerequisites* to components search?

- The technique is applicable, primarily, in assembly operations (but also in process-oriented operations, where there are several similar processes or machines), where the larger the difference in output between the two units, the better.
- The performance (output) must be measurable and repeatable.
- The units must be capable of disassembly and reassembly without a significant change in the original output.
- There must be at least two assemblies or systems with clearly different levels of the output. For brevity, the two assemblies are described as "good" and "bad," but there need not be a "bad" unit as such.

The *procedure* to be followed in components search involves ten steps:

1. Select the best and the worst performing unit from, say, a day's production.
2. Determine the quantitative parameter by which good and bad units are to be measured. Measure both units and note the readings.
3. Disassemble the good unit twice. Reassemble and remeasure it each time. Disassemble the bad unit twice. Reassemble and remeasure it. The three good unit readings must all rank better than all three bad units and the difference, D, between the *medians* of the good and bad units must exceed the average range $\bar{d}$, (where $\bar{d}$ is the range, of nonrepeatability within each of the good builds

and bad builds respectively), by a minimum ratio of 1.25:1. Only then can a significant and repeatable difference between the good and bad units be established (see case study on the hourmeter, this chapter).

4. Based upon engineering knowledge of the design of the system, rank the component names in descending order of perceived importance.

5. Switch the top-ranked component from the good unit or assembly with the corresponding component in the bad assembly. Measure the two assemblies.

6(a). If there is no change, i.e., if the good assembly stays good and the bad assembly stays bad within calculated control limits, the top component, A, is unimportant. Go to component B.

  (b). If there is a partial change out of the control limits for one or both of the two assembly outputs, A is not the only important variable. A is important but not alone. Further, A's interaction effects with other components cannot be ruled out. Go to component B.

  (c). If there is a complete reversal in the outputs of the two assemblies, A would be the part having a Red X quality characteristic. There is no further need for components search.

7. In each of the three alternatives in Step 6, restore component A to the original good and bad units (before Step 5) to ensure that the original condition is repeated. Repeat Steps 5 and 6 with the next most important component, B, then C, then D, etc., if the results in each component swap are 6(a) or 6(b).

8. Ultimately, the Red X family involving two or more components will be indicated. If there are two or more significant changes, a Red X interaction could be found in the Step 10 analysis.

9. With the important components identified, a capping run of these important components banded

together in the good and bad assemblies must be conducted to verify their importance.

10. Finally, a factorial matrix, using the data generated in Steps 2, 6, and 7, is drawn to determine, quantitatively, main effects and interaction effects. Steps 9 and 10 are best explained using a real-life case study.

Components Search Case Study: The Hourmeter

An hourmeter, built by an electronics company, had a 20–25 percent defect rate because several of the units could not meet the customer's reliability requirement of perfect operation at $-40°C$. The worst units could only reach 0°C before malfunction.

The hourmeter consists of a solenoid cell with a shield to concentrate the electrical charge which pulses at regular intervals. The pulse triggers a solenoid pin, which in turn causes a verge arm, or bell crank, to trip the counter, advancing it by one unit. The counter is attached to a numeral shaft containing numeral wheels. These numeral wheels are separated from each other by idler gears, which rotate on an idler gear shaft. Both the idler gear shaft and the numeral shaft are attached to the mainframe, made of hard white plastic. The pulsing rhythm is provided by an electronics board.

Establishing Significant Repeatable Differences

	High (Good) Assembly	Low (Bad) Assembly
Initial results	OK at ($H1$): $-40°C$	($L1$): 0°C
Results after 1st disassembly/ reassembly	OK at ($H2$): $-35°C$	($L2$): $-5°C$
Results after 2nd disassembly/ reassembly	OK at ($H3$): $-37°C$	($L3$): $-7°C$

The test for a significant and repeatable difference between the good units and bad units is determined by the
formula:

$$D:\bar{d} \geq 1.25:1$$

That is, the ratio of D to $\bar{d}$ should be a minimum of 1.25:1,
based on the 0.05 level classical F table with three builds of
each assembly, where D = the differences between the median results of the two assemblies, and $\bar{d}$ = (range of nonrepeatability of the high assembly + range of nonrepeatability
of the low assembly)/2.

In the above replication, the medians of the high and low
assemblies are $-37°C$ and $-5°C$. Therefore $D = -37° - (-5°) = -32°$.

$$\bar{d} = - \{(40 - 35) + (7 - 0)\}/2 = - 6°.$$

So $D:\bar{d} = - 32: - 6 = 5.33:1$, which exceeds the minimum 1.25:1 ratio.

Conclusion. (1) All three high assemblies outrank all
three low assemblies; (2) the minimum ratio of $D:\bar{d} \geq 1.25:1$
has been met; (3) Stage 1, therefore, is successful. The Red X
and Pink X are among the causes being considered and there
is good repeatability in the disassembly/reassembly process.

Ranking of Components by Importance

(Engineering Judgment)

Rank	Components	Label
1	Solenoid, pin, and shield	A
2	Idler gear shaft	B
3	Numeral shaft	C
4	Mainframe	D
5	Bell crank	E
6	Idler gears	F
7	Numeral wheels	G
8	Circuit board	H
9	Remainder of components	R (Remainder)

Testing Symbols

A_{LRH} = A from low (bad) unit, with remainder of components, R, from high (good) unit

A_{HRL} = A from high (good) unit, with remainder of components, R, from low (bad) unit

etc.

Capping Run and Control Limits

This is a concluding test, where the high (good) levels of the important components are tested with the low (bad) levels of the remaining components, and vice versa, to see if a complete reversal takes place. If it does, the important components are captured and the remainder, as a group, can be reduced in cost.

When one component is swapped, there can be a very great number of possible interactions simultaneously "created" that involve that component. Control limits are used to determine whether a component and its associated interaction effects are important (outside of the control limits) or unimportant (inside the control limits) and eliminated.

The control limits for each new swapped result are given by the formula:

$$\text{control limits} = \text{median} \pm t_{0.95}\, \overline{d} / d_2$$

where t is the value corresponding to a 0.95 or 95 percent confidence and $\overline{d} / d_2$ is an estimate of σ. With three disassemblies/reassemblies for both the good and bad units, we have 2 degrees of freedom for each of them, or a total of 4 degrees of freedom. From the student's t table,* with 4 degrees of freedom, t—for a 2-tailed 95 percent confidence—is 2.776. d_2 is the statistical constant of 1.81.

Therefore control limits = median ± 2.776 $\overline{d}$ / 1.81.

*See J. Duncan Acheson, *Quality Control and Industrial Statistics*, 5th ed. (Homewood, Ill.: Richard D. Irwin Inc., 1986), p. 1007, Table D3.

Test Results

After initial and two replication tests, each component is swapped, one at a time, between high (good) and low (bad) assemblies. Table 7-2 shows the result of Stages 1, 2, and 3 of the components search study on the hourmeter.

The control limits for the middle "results" column are −27.8° and −46.2°. Only tests 4 and 7 show results out of control. The limits for the end "results" column are −4.2° and −14.2°. All the test number results were in control. Remember, the component is significant if *one or both* of the interchanged results are out of control.

Figure 7-1 is a graphical representation of the test results. It shows the clear separation between the original high (good) and low (bad) assemblies, as well as their replicated versions (disassembled and reassembled). The graph shows a partial convergence between the high and low assemblies when components D (mainframe) and G (numeral wheels) are switched. The contribution of the remaining components is minor or zero.

In the capping run, when the two Pink X components, D and G, are combined at low levels, with all other components at high levels, the results are bad. When D and G are combined at high levels, with all other components at low levels, the results are good. The graph shows a complete reversal of high and low, indicating that the family of the Red X is narrowed down to D and G, that all other components are unimportant, that further components search can be discontinued, and that the tolerances of the remaining components may be opened up if realistic tolerance plots justify them (see Chapter 12).

Factorial Analysis

The purpose of a factorial analysis is to determine, quantitatively, the importance of each major factor previously identified in a components search, variables search, or full

Table 7-2. Components search: the hourmeter experiment.

Test No.	Component Switched	High Assembly	Results	Control* Limits	Low Assembly	Results	Control* Limits	Analysis
Initial No. 1 Disassembly/Reassembly		All Comp. High	-40°		All Comp. Low	0°		
No. 2 Disassembly/Reassembly		All Comp. High	-35°		All Comp. Low	-5°		
		All Comp. High	-37°		All Comp. Low	-7°		
1	A	$A_L R_H$	-40°	-27.8° and -46.2°	$A_H R_L$	-5°	-14.2° and +4.2°	A Unimportant
2	B	$B_L R_H$	-35°	-27.8° and -46.2°	$B_H R_L$	0°	-14.2° and +4.2°	B Unimportant
3	C	$C_L R_H$	-35°	-27.8° and -46.2°	$C_H R_L$	-5°	-14.2° and +4.2°	C Unimportant
4	D	$D_L R_H$	-20°	-27.8° and -46.2°	$D_H R_L$	-5°	-14.2° and +4.2°	D Important
5	E	$E_L R_H$	-40°	-27.8° and -46.2°	$E_H R_L$	0°	-14.2° and +4.2°	E Unimportant
6	F	$F_L R_H$	-40°	-27.8° and -46.2°	$F_H R_L$	-5°	-14.2° and +4.2°	F Unimportant
7	G	$G_L R_H$	-20°	-27.8° and -46.2°	$G_H R_L$	-5°	-14.2° and +4.2°	G Important
8	H	$H_L R_H$	-35°	-27.8° and -46.2°	$H_H R_L$	0°	-14.2° and +4.2°	H Unimportant
Capping Run	D and G	$D_L G_L R_H$	0°	-27.8° and -46.2°	$D_H G_H R_L$	-40°	-14.2° and +4.2°	D and G Important

*Control Limits = Median $\pm \bar{d}/1.81$

Median for High Assemblies = -37°; Median for Low Assemblies = -5°

$\bar{d}$ = (Range for High Assemblies + Range for Low Assemblies)/2 = $(7+5)/2 = 6$

Control Limits (High Side) = -37° ±6/1.81 = 27.8° and -46.2°

Control Limits (Low Side) = 5° ±6/1.81 = -4.2° and -14.2°

CONCLUSION:

1. Components A, B, C, E, F, and H are within the high side and low side control limits. So they are *unimportant*.
2. Components D and G are outside the high side control limits. So they are *important*.
3. The capping run confirmed that D and G combined go outside both sides of the control limits. So D and G and their interaction effects are important.

Figure 7-1. Hourmeter experiment: a graphical plot.

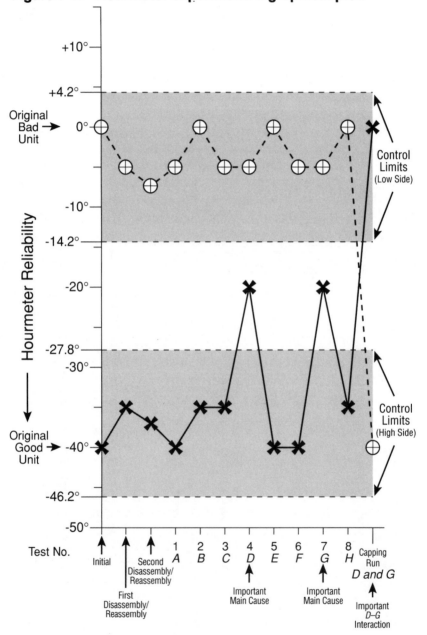

factorial experiment, and to quantify the interaction effects between such factors as they affect a desired output.

Main Effects and Interaction Effects

Before a factorial analysis can be explained, it is necessary to understand main effects and interaction effects. A simple analogy will help. Take two numbers, 3 and 7. Their sum is 10. Numbers 3 and 7 can be called independent variables, each contributing independently to the result of 10, which can be called a main effect. However, 3 + 7 can also produce a different number in the physical world (though not in mathematics), like 16, where the whole is greater than the sum of the parts. This is called an interaction effect, which is additive to any significant main effects. There is a synergy, a symbiotic relationship between the two independent variables 3 and 7.

On the other hand, 3 and 7 can also result in +4 or in −4, still main effects, or in 2, an interaction effect.

There are many examples of interaction effects. For instance, alcohol alone and drugs alone may not necessarily create lasting injury (unless taken in excess); but if a person takes both at the same time, the result can be fatal. That is an interaction effect. Another example would be hydrogen and oxygen. Strike a match in either by itself and nothing happens. But with the right mixture of the two, an explosion will occur when the match is lit. This phenomenon is a classic example of an interaction effect. In the world of human relations, there are similar interaction effects. Ordinary people, working and pulling together, often achieve extraordinary results. The world of sports, where teams have been "fired up," often has additive interaction effects. On the other hand, in the field of politics and in industry, with people "bucking" one another, we see almost a checkmate condition due to subtractive interaction effects.

In the design of experiments, it is necessary to quantify not only the main effects of each important factor, but also the interaction effects between these important factors or variables. This is best done in a factorial analysis, as shown in Figure 7-2 for the components search in the hourmeter case study.

Because component D, the mainframe, and component G, the numeral wheels, are the only two factors that showed a partial reversal during components search and a full reversal when switched together, they can be called two equal (not usual) Red X main effects and, as you will see, a Pink X (smaller magnitude) DG interaction.

To quantify the main and interaction effects of factors D and G, the matrix in Figure 7-2 must be drawn up. First, the outputs when both D and G are low should be entered from the test results. The first reading, $0°$, is from the initial "low assembly," where D and G are both "low." The second, $-5°$, and the third, $-7°$, are from the replicated low assembly. The fourth, fifth, and sixth readings of $-5°$, $0°$, and $-5°$ are from the low assemblies in tests 1, 2, and 3, as are the seventh, eighth, and tenth readings of $0°$, $-5°$, and $0°$ from the low assemblies in tests 5, 6, and 8. The last test where D and G are both low is in the capping run (with R_H = remaining components high). That reading is $0°$. In similar fashion, there are two readings where D is high and G is low; two readings where D is low and G is high; and ten readings where both D and G are high. The average for each cell is then calculated.

In the factorial matrix of Figure 7-2, if the averages in the D_L column are added up and those in the D_H column also added, the difference between these additions divided by 2 gives the contribution of factor D alone to the output. This happens because, in the addition of the two D_L and D_H columns, G_L and G_H balance each other (or cancel out). This is called the main effect of factor D. Similarly, adding up the averages in the G_L and G_H rows and dividing their difference by 2 gives the contribution of factor G alone. Here D_L and D_H balance each other. This is called the main effect of factor G. Finally, when the averages in the diagonal from cell $D_H G_L$ to $D_L G_H$ are added and the averages in the diagonal from cell $D_L G_H$ to $D_H G_L$ are also added, the difference between these sums divided by 2 gives the contribution of the D and G interaction alone to the output.

Figure 7-2. Factorial analysis.

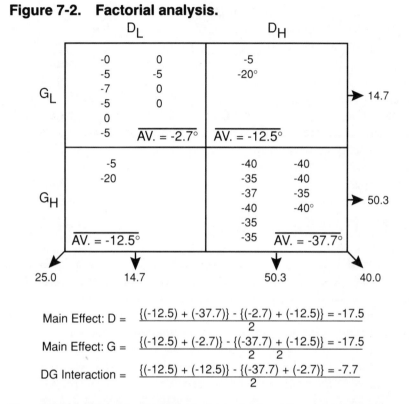

Main Effect: D = $\dfrac{\{(-12.5) + (-37.7)\} - \{(-2.7) + (-12.5)\}}{2} = -17.5$

Main Effect: G = $\dfrac{\{(-12.5) + (-2.7)\} - \{(-37.7) + (-12.5)\}}{2 \quad 2} = -17.5$

DG Interaction = $\dfrac{\{(-12.5) + (-12.5)\} - \{(-37.7) + (-2.7)\}}{2} = -7.7$

The confidence in the main effects and the interaction is not the same because the number of data behind the results is different.

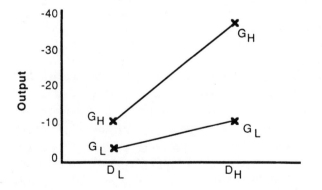

Figure 7-2 also shows a graphical plot of the DG interaction effect. The G_LD_L reading of $-2.7°$ is plotted, as are the remaining three readings of D_LG_H at $-12.5°$, D_HG_L at $-12.5°$, and D_HG_H at $-37.7°$. When these four points are connected by two lines, G_L and G_H, there is a nonparallel effect indicating the presence of a reasonably strong interaction between factors D and G. (If the lines had been parallel, the interpretation would be that D and G produce main effects only with no interaction present.)

The Final Solution to the Hourmeter Case Study

Table 7-3 is a summary of the final solution to which components search pointed the way. *As a result, the defect rate went from the 20–25 percent range down to zero!*

The reliability engineer who conducted the components search study wrote the following postscript to his report:

> The problem had been with us for 18 months. We had talked to suppliers; we had talked to engineers and designers; we had talked to engineering managers; *but we never talked to the parts. With the components search technique, we identified the problem in just three days!*

Practice Exercise on Components Search: Time Delay

An electronic instrument has a problem of a long time delay between the "power on" signal and when the unit actually starts to function. A "good" unit has a time delay of around 16 milliseconds (ms), while a "bad" unit has one of 30 ms. The oscillator circuit containing ten components was the source of the delay. The following components search was conducted. (R = rest of assembly)

			Results			Results
Test No.	*Component Switched*	*High Assembly*	*(ms)*	*Low Assembly*	*(ms)*
Initial	—	All Comp. High	13	All Comp. Low	34
No. 1 Disassembly and Reassembly	—	All Comp. High	16	All Comp. Low	38
No. 2 Disassembly and Reassembly	—	All Comp. High	15	All Comp. Low	35

Table 7-3.   Final solution to hourmeter case study.

ANALYSIS OF EXPERIMENT

- Mainframe and numeral wheels causing drop in performance

ENGINEERING ANALYSIS

- 60 × life-size model built
- Isolated *first* numeral wheel and mainframe as problem
- Made measurements at critical points at different temperatures

RESULTS

- Mainframe shrunk by up to 0.002″, bringing numeral wheel and idler shaft too close
- First numeral wheel off center by 0.005″
- Counter jammed when shrinkage coincided with eccentricity

SOLUTION

- Redesign mainframe (cost $50,000)
- *Or* change numeral wheel specification and tolerance (low cost)
- Second alternative selected

POSTSCRIPT

- Yields rose from 75–80% to 100%

1	A = crystal	A_LR_H	16	A_HR_L	19
2	B = microprocessor	B_LR_H	16	B_HR_L	35
3	C = transistor	C_LR_H	14	C_HR_L	33
4	D = capacitor C_2	D_LR_H	15	D_HR_L	37
5	E = capacitor C_1	E_LR_H	16	E_HR_L	18
Capping Run	A and E	$A_LE_LR_H$	32	$A_HE_HR_L$	17

Question 1. Stage 1. Determine if there is a significant and repeatable difference between the high and low assemblies in the initial and replicated (after disassembly and assembly) tests.

Question 2. Stage 2. Plot the results listed in the above table. Calculate the control limits. What are the unimportant components?

Question 3. Stage 3. Was the capping run successful?

Question 4. Stage 4. Construct a factorial analysis. Determine the main and interaction effects of the important components. Construct a graphical plot to show the extent of interaction.

The answers to the exercise on components search follow:

Question 1. Stage 1. (1) The three high assemblies all outrank the three low assemblies. The medians of the high and low assemblies are 15 and 35.

Therefore, $D = 35 - 15 = 20$

The ranges in each of the high assemblies and low assemblies are 3 and 4 respectively.

Therefore, $\bar{d} = (3+4)/2 = 3.5$

(2) So D: $\bar{d} = 20{:}3.5 = 5.71{:}1$, which exceeds the minimum 1.25:1 ratio.

Stage 1 is, therefore, successful.

Question 2. Stage 2. The control limits are: median $\pm$ 2.776 $\bar{d}$ / 1.81 (= median $\pm$ 5.37). For the high readings, the control limits are: $35 \pm 5.37 = 40.37$ and 29.63. For the low readings, the control limits are: $15 \pm 5.37 = 20.37$ and 9.63. Components A and E are beyond the control limits among the high readings. No components are beyond the control limits among the low readings.

Conclusion. Only the components A and E, that is, the crystal and capacitor C_1, are important and their interaction effect must be determined. The rest of the components and their associated interaction effects can be eliminated.

Question 3. Stage 3. The capping run is successful. With AE paired high and the remaining components R low and vice versa, the results are beyond the control limits.

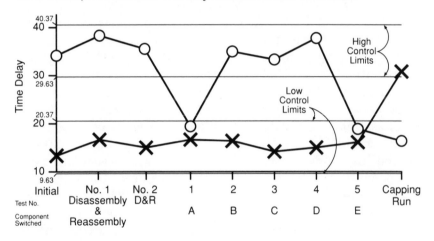

It was determined that the capping run was successful. Use factorial analysis and determine the contrasts. What are your conclusions?

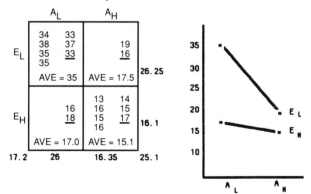

MAIN EFFECT   A $= \dfrac{17.5 + 15.1}{2} - \dfrac{35 + 17}{2} = 9.7$ Pink *X*

MAIN EFFECT   E $= \dfrac{17 + 15.1}{2} - \dfrac{35 + 17.5}{2} = 10.2$ Red *X*

INTERACTION   AE $= \dfrac{15.1 + 35}{2} - \dfrac{17 + 17.5}{2} = 7.8$ Pale Pink *X*

CONCLUSION: An important interaction does exist
               as well as two important main effects:

Question 4. Stage 4. The factorial analysis shows that factors *A* and *E* contribute 9.5 ms and 10.15 ms, respectively, to the total variations in delay, while the *AE* interaction contributes 7.9 ms. The graphical plot shows a strong interaction (nonparallel response) between *A* and *E*.

The above exercise is based on an actual case study. Engineering investigation revealed that the series impedance of the crystal was on the low side and the capacitor leakage on the high side. When this condition was present in both components, the oscillator circuit loaded down the microprocessor, causing a long time delay. Working with the capacitor supplier (using DOE), the investigators of the components search were able to reduce leakage at no extra cost and to resolve the time delay.

8

Paired Comparisons: The Detective Method

Objective, Application, Procedure

The paired comparisons method is similar to components search, with the objective of reducing a large number of possible causes of variation down to the family of the Red X by providing clues derived from comparisons of paired "good" and "bad" units.

The technique is used when:

- Components or subassemblies in units cannot be disassembled or reassembled (unlike components search)
- There are several good and a few bad units that can be paired
- A suitable parameter can be found to distinguish good from bad

The technique is applicable in assembly work or processes or in test equipment, where there are similar units, workstations, or instruments, respectively. It is also a powerful tool in failure analysis.

The procedure to be followed in paired comparisons involves five steps:

1. Select one good unit and one bad unit (drawn, where possible, close to the same production time).
2. Call this pair one. Observe in detail to note differences between these two units. The differences can be visual, dimensional, electrical, mechanical, chemical, etc. The observation techniques could involve the eye, X rays, scanning electron microscopes, test-to-destruction, etc.
3. Select a second pair of good and bad units. Observe and note the differences, as in Step 2.
4. Repeat this search process with a third, fourth, fifth, and sixth pair, until the observed differences show a pattern of repeatability.
5. Disregard differences that show contrary directions among the pairs. Usually, by the fifth or sixth pair, the consistent differences will be narrowed down to a few factors, providing a strong clue for the major cause of variation.

Paired Comparisons Case Study: The Failed Diode

A DO-35 diode, used in an under-the-hood electronics module in an automobile, had an unacceptable failure rate. Several of the failed diodes were brought back from the field and compared against good units that had no flaws. The results of the paired comparisons, when examined under a scanning electron microscope, were as follows:

Pair No.		*Observed Differences*
1. Good-Bad	Good:	No flaws
	Bad:	Chipped die, oxide defects, copper migration
2. Good-Bad	Good:	No flaws
	Bad:	Alloying irregularities, oxide defects
3. Good-Bad	Good:	No flaws
	Bad:	Oxide defects, contamination
4. Good-Bad	Good:	No flaws
	Bad:	Oxide defects, chipped die

Conclusion:

1. Four repeats in oxide defects, probable Red X family
2. Two repeats in chipped die, probable Pink X family

Solution: Working with the semiconductor supplier (who, up to this analysis, had resisted responsibility), the following corrective actions were instituted:

1. For oxide defects:
   - Thicker photo resist
   - Mask inspection
   - Increased separation between mask and die
2. For chipped die:
   - Reduced oxide thickness in scribe grid

Practice Exercise on Paired Comparisons: Crystal Drop Test

A 12 MHz crystal was failing to meet a reliability requirement when subjected to a drop test from a height of one meter. Because the crystal could not be disassembled and reassembled, components search could not be used. Paired comparisons appeared to be the right technique. Several failed samples were collected and compared against good crystals (which had passed the drop test) for consistent external differences. None were found. It was decided, then, to x-ray each pair of good and bad units, with the following results.

Pair No.	*Observed Differences*	
1. Good-Bad	Good:	Straight post
	Bad:	Post tilted 10° from vertical
2. Good-Bad	Good:	Straight post
	Bad:	Post tilted 5° from vertical
3. Good-Bad	Good:	Straight post
	Bad:	Post tilted 20° from vertical
4. Good-Bad	Good:	Straight post
	Bad:	Post tilted 10° from vertical

Question 1. What is the observable, repeatable difference between the good and bad crystals?

Question 2. Does the difference need to be validated by further tests?

These are the answers to the exercise on paired comparisons:

Question 1. The observable difference is obvious: tilted posts.

Question 2. A B vs. C test (see Chapter 11) was set up to determine if preselected crystals with straight posts (*B* unit) would outperform preselected crystals with tilted posts (*C* units) in further drop tests. The result: The crystals with tilted posts all failed within one meter in drop tests. The crystals with straight posts did not fail even up to two meters.

The solution was that a new automated crystal assembler was used by the crystal supplier to properly frame the mounting post of the crystal base and insert the crystal wafer.

9

Variables Search: The Rolls-Royce of Variation Reduction

The systematic reduction of variation starts with a multi-vari chart, a components search, or a paired comparison (or sometimes two or all three of these techniques done sequentially or simultaneously), where the aim is to reduce a very large number of unrelated causes down to a smaller family of related causes, generally five to fifteen. Variables search is the next step. Its *objectives* are to (1) pinpoint the Red X, Pink X, and, sometimes, one to three more interacting variables (because it is possible that a strong interaction between two variables may itself be the Red X or Pink X) and (2) separate the important variables from the unimportant ones, tightly control the former, and open up the tolerances on the latter in order to reduce costs.

Principle and Application

One of the important principles in DOE is to design an experiment so that every variable is tested with each level of every other variable. As an example, if eight variables are the possible causes in the variation of a given output, and two levels of each variable are considered, there are 2^8 or 256 combinations of possible tests. Only a full factorial experiment (explained in Chapter 10) can test all these combinations with neatly separated and quantified interaction effects. But a full factorial with 256 experiments would be very costly and time-consuming. Hence various shortcuts have been applied, such as the fractional factorial design in the classical approach and the orthogonal array in the Taguchi approach. However, as explained in the Appendix, both these approaches have such a hit-and-miss method of selecting only a few combinations, such as 16 or 32, out of the total of 256 that the results are modest and often inaccurate, especially if interactions are present.

Variables search overcomes this difficulty *by a homing-in binary technique, through a process of elimination.* The *principle* is similar to that explained in components search. In fact, the second stage of a variables search experiment is a components search. Thus, 256 or 512 or 1,024 or 2,048 combinations can be reduced to yield Red X or Pink X culprits in 10 to 30 experiments! It is small wonder that variables search is called the Rolls-Royce of DOE techniques.

Variables search is most *applicable* when there are five or more variables to investigate. While there is no theoretical upper limit, practical considerations limit the number of variables to a range from five to fifteen. Further, the output must be measurable—a variable, preferably, although a solution for attribute outputs has now been developed. Finally, in the choice of "high" and "low" levels, it is advisable to know and to quantify "high" and "low" in advance. This is explained in the procedure below.

The principles and practice of variables search are similar to the ones described in components search (Chapter 7). Components search deals with discrete components or parts, whereas variables search deals with both products and processes, even where swapping the same part is not possible.

Procedure in Variables Search

Stage 1

1. List the most important input variables or factors or causes (these are all synonymous terms): *A, B, C, D, E, F, G,*

H, and so on, in *descending order of importance* of each factor's ability to influence the output.

- The selection is best made with a prior multi-vari, components search, or paired comparisons study determining *the family of likely factors.*
- If, however, the product or process is new, at the prototype stage of design, and there are not sufficient quantities to run a multi-vari, components search, or paired comparisons study, then:
    — Use a computer simulation to select the important or likely factors. (It must be remembered, however, that a computer is only as good as the formula used to program it. In many complex products or processes, the formula that governs the relationship between independent input variables and a dependent output is not known, in which case the mighty computer is reduced to guesswork! Even if the formula is known, it is always desirable to confirm the results of a computer simulation with a hardware variables search experiment.)
    — Conduct a brainstorming session, using engineering, operator, and maintenance personnel inputs, to generate a list of likely factors.

2. Assign two levels to each factor: a high, which is most likely to contribute to good (or even the best) results, and a low, which represents a most likely deviation from the high level in day-to-day production with normal maintenance. (Sometimes, the sign $(+)$ is assigned to each high level and the sign $(-)$ to each low level.) If variables search is conducted in the prototype design stage, the low level is an engineering judgment of how far the factor differs from the high or best level to register a large repeatable difference, within practical limits. If the experimenters (usually a team representing engineering, manufacturing, and quality) are not sure about which level, high or low, is better, they can assign high and low levels arbitrarily. The variables search experiment will determine, in subsequent stages, which level is better.

3. Run two experiments, one with all factors at their high levels, the other with all factors at their low levels.

Repeat these two experiments twice more, so that there are three runs with all high levels and three runs with all low levels. To avoid the effect of nonrandomization and the consequent biased readings that may result, randomize the sequence of these six texts, using a random number table (see Chapter 10) or equivalent. Running all three high levels first and all three low levels next, or vice versa, *may* not give uncontrollable causes an equal chance of entering into or departing from the experiments.

4. Apply the $D: \bar{d} \geq 1.25{:}1$ rule, as seen in the components search study, where D is the difference between the mean of the high readings and the mean of the low readings and $\bar{d}$ is the average of the differences in repeatability within each set of high and low readings.

5. Stage 1 is over when (a) all three high levels are better than (in rank order) all three low levels (i.e., an end count of 6; see Chapter 11) and (b) where the $D{:}\bar{d}$ ratio is $\geq 1.25{:}1$. If all three high levels are worse than (in rank order) all three low levels, just change the headings of high to low and vice versa.

6. If either of the two conditions (a) and (b) is not met, then switch one pair of the most likely factors from high to low and vice versa to see if a cancellation of influence was taking place. If there is still no significant difference, switch a second pair of factors. Generally, if the factors in Step 1 have been carefully selected, say, through a multi-vari study, Step 6 should not be necessary. At most, it may be only one or two factors where the engineering judgment of high and low levels may have been reversed.

7. If the repeatability, $\bar{d}$, in Step 4 is still poor, it is an indication that an important factor has been left out in Step 1. Look for a clue as to one or more factors to be added to the list in Step 1 and rerun Stage 1.

8. At first glance, Stage 1 may appear to the novice as lengthy and complicated. But in hundreds of applications of variables search, Stage 1 results are generally quick and positive, not requiring the further probing of Steps 6 or 7.

Stage 2 (Elimination)

1. Run a pair of tests (1) with the low level of the most important factor, A, i.e., A_L, along with the high levels of all the remaining factors labeled R_H; (2) with the high level of the most important factor, A, i.e., A_H, along with the low levels of all the remaining factors labeled R_L. Calculate the high side and low side control limits, using the same formula as in components search.

The control limits are: median $\pm$ 2.776 ($\overline{d}$ / 1.81).

Possible Results

(a) If both pairs of tests—i.e., A_LR_H and A_HR_L—show results *inside* the low side and high side control limits, respectively, factor A, along with all of its associated interaction effects, is unimportant and can be eliminated from further study.

(b) If there is a complete reversal, i.e., if A_LR_H becomes the original all-high level and A_HR_L becomes the original all-low level, A is a main effect Red X. The rest of the factors—B, C, D, etc.—are all unimportant and can be eliminated. Variables search has ended.

(c) If either or both pairs of tests, A_LR_H and A_HR_L, show results *outside* the low side and high side control limits, respectively, but not a complete reversal, factor A, along with its associated interaction effects, cannot be eliminated. A plus some other factor or factors must be considered.

2. If the results in Step 1 are (a) or (c), repeat Step 1 with factor B. If (a) results, B is unimportant and can be eliminated. If (b) results, B is the Red X; end of variables search. If (c) results, B cannot be eliminated. B plus some other factor or factors must be considered.

3. If the result in Step 2 is (a), repeat Step 1 with factor C. If (a) results, C is unimportant and can be eliminated. If (b) results, C is the Red X; end of variables search. If (c) results, C cannot be eliminated. C plus some other factor or factors must be considered.

Stage 3 (Capping Run)

1. If factors A and B display a partial reversal (result c), with readings *outside* the control limits, run a capping run with these factors, $A_H B_H R_L$ and $A_L B_L R_H$, to see if R, the rest of the factors, can be eliminated. One or more results *outside* of the complete *reversal* control limits would indicate that the search is not yet complete. Continue (Stage 2) with the next single factors in alphabetical order until another factor shows out-of-control result(s).

2. Now run a three-factor capping run. (Generally going to a four-factor capping run is rare.)

Stage 4 (Factorial Analysis)

Finally, draw up a factorial analysis* using the data generated in Stage 1 and Stage 2, similar to the technique explained in the case study on components search (Chapter 7), to quantify the main effects and interaction effects of the important factors.

Post—Variables Search

Make every attempt to maintain the important factors at their best levels when production starts (or for subsequent production runs) by:

1. Reducing and controlling supplier variability of the important components (and simultaneously getting a price decrease from the supplier based on his higher yields)
2. Redesigning, reducing, and controlling process variability of the important components

*If the factorial analysis involves three or four factors that cannot be eliminated in Stage 2, the factorial analysis can be similar to a full factorial table (without the necessity for an actual experiment; see Chapter 10, Table 10-2).

3. Maintaining reduced process variability through Positrol (see Chapter 16)

Conduct further experiments, scatter plots (Chapter 12), (1) to determine how far the tolerances of the unimportant components can be opened, especially if there is an appreciable cost reduction benefit; (2) to find the optimum center of values for the important components and the maximum tolerances permissible, to achieve a minimum of C_{pk} of 2 for the output.

Uses of Variables Search

In cases where variations or defects exist in only a small percentage of units, get the important clues from paired comparisons for the variables $A, B, C,$ etc., in order to conduct a variables search experiment.

Where disassembly is not possible, the Stage 1 procedure is not changed. But in Stage 2 the sample size may have to be increased and brand-new units used for the $A_W R_B, A_B R_W$ combinations, etc. Although this may not give as accurate a result as a direct interchange, the main and interaction effects will still show up in a very pronounced manner.

To summarize, variables search:

- Reduces product/process variability far more than do the classical approach or the Taguchi approach to the design of experiments, and also gives more dependable, repeatable results.
- Is an ideal DOE tool for separating the important variables from the unimportant ones. By closely controlling the important variables, it goes beyond zero defects toward zero variation, with tremendous savings in the costs of poor quality. By opening up tolerances on the unimportant variables, it is also a powerful cost reduction tool.
- Utilizes a method so simple that it can be performed by

technicians and line workers with little statistical knowledge.
- Economizes the cost of experimentation by factors of 3:1 and up to 10:1 over classical and Taguchi DOE experiments.

Variables Search Case Study: The Press Brake

In a metal stamping/forming operation, parts produced on the press brakes could not be held to a ± 0.005″ tolerance (or process width of 0.010″). Tolerances as high as ± 0.010″ were being measured some of the time in production. The press brake was perceived to be a temperamental operation, in the "black magic" category, requiring the use of highly skilled operators to get consistent results. The causes of the large variation (C_{pk}s down to 0.5) were hotly debated, answers ranging from supplier material (inconsistent thickness and/or inconsistent hardness) to press brake parameters that could not be controlled. Efforts to experiment with newer press brakes, with much higher capital costs, had not resulted in any significant quality improvement.

A variables search experiment was then tried. The objective was to bring the process under control, consistently, to ± 0.005″ or closer. Six factors were selected, in descending order of perceived importance, and the high and low levels for each factor determined. (In the interest of protecting confidential information, the precise levels used are not mentioned. They are labeled merely in general quantitative terms.) The six factors chosen, together with the Stage 1 and Stage 2 results, are shown in Table 9-1 and analyzed in Figure 9-1.

Conclusions

As a result of the variables search experiment:

- The parts tolerances on the brake could be held to ± 0.002" (process width of 0.004″)—better than twice the original objective.

Table 9-1. Variables search: the press brake case study.

Factors	High	Low
A. Punch and die alignment	Aligned	Not aligned
B. Metal thickness	Thick	Thin
C. Metal hardness	Hard	Soft
D. Metal bow	Flat	Bowed
E. Ram stroke	Coin form	Air form
F. Holding material	Level	At angle

Results. Numbers below are expressed in deviation from nominal in multiples of 0.001". (Low tolerances are better and vice versa.)

STAGE 1	All High Levels	All Low Levels
Initial	4	47
1st Replication	4	61
2nd Replication	3	68

STAGE 2

Test	Combination	Results	Median	Control Limits	Conclusion
1	$A_L R_H$	3	4	-12.87 to 20.87	A Not important
2	$A_H R_L$	72	61	44.13 to 77.87	
3	$B_L R_H$	5	4	-12.87 to 20.87	B Not important
4	$B_H R_L$	47	61	44.13 to 77.87	
5	$C_L R_H$	7	4	-12.87 to 20.87	C Not Important
6	$C_H R_L$	72	61	44.13 to 77.87	
7	$D_L R_H$	23	4	-12.87 to 20.87	D Important with
8	$D_H R_L$	30	61	44.13 to 77.87	another factor
9	$E_L R_H$	7	4	-12.87 to 20.87	E Not important
10	$E_H R_L$	50	61	44.13 to 77.87	
11	$F_L R_H$	73	4	-12.87 to 20.87	F Important with
12	$R_H R_L$	18	61	44.13 to 77.87	another factor
Capping Run	$D_L F_L R_H$	70	4	-12.87 to 20.87	• DF interaction important
Capping Run	$D_H F_H R_L$	4	61	44.13 to 77.87	• Complete reversal • End of test

*Medians for high and low assemblies are 4 and 61 respectively; so D = 61–4 = 57
$\bar{d}$ = Average lack of repeatability in each assembly = (1 + 21)/2 = 11
So $D/\bar{d}$ = 57:11 = 5.2:1, which is greater than 1.25:1. So Stage 1 is successful,
Control Limits = Median $\pm 2.776 \bar{d}/1.81$ = Median ± 16.87
So Control Limits (High Side) = 44.13 to 77.87
So Control Limits (Low Side) = –12.87 to 20.87

Figure 9-1.   Factorial analysis (see the case study on components search in Chapter 7 for a full explanation of factorial analysis).

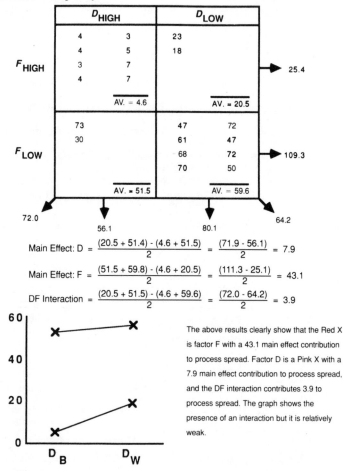

Main Effect: D $= \dfrac{(20.5 + 51.4) - (4.6 + 51.5)}{2} = \dfrac{(71.9 - 56.1)}{2} = 7.9$

Main Effect: F $= \dfrac{(51.5 + 59.8) - (4.6 + 20.5)}{2} = \dfrac{(111.3 - 25.1)}{2} = 43.1$

DF Interaction $= \dfrac{(20.5 + 51.5) - (4.6 + 59.6)}{2} = \dfrac{(72.0 - 64.2)}{2} = 3.9$

The above results clearly show that the Red X is factor F with a 43.1 main effect contribution to process spread. Factor D is a Pink X with a 7.9 main effect contribution to process spread, and the DF interaction contributes 3.9 to process spread. The graph shows the presence of an interaction but it is relatively weak.

- The C_{pk} was increased from an unacceptable 0.5 to a comfortable 2.5 (0.010/0.004) with just one experiment.
- The material thickness and hardness were no longer thought to be important considerations and so the tolerances on these parameters could be opened up. The bow in the material was the important parameter to control.
- A fixture was devised to keep the holding material (Red

X) always level, thus eliminating operator-controlled variations.

Practice Exercise on Variables Search:
Engine Control Module

A microprocessor-based engine control module had to meet an important specification for idle speed current. The specification limits were from 650 milliamperes to 800 ma. There was a reject rate of 10–12 percent in pilot run production. Appeals to the car company for a relaxation of the specification were to no avail. If the idle speed current went below 650 ma, the car company claimed, the car might not start. If it went above 800 ma, some of the components could burn up.

A variables search experiment was in order. Engineering selected seven factors, in descending order of importance, that could affect the output, i.e., idle speed current. These are shown in Table 9-2. The high levels for each factor were deemed to be at the design center value of each component. The low levels were judged to be at one end or the other of the tolerances specified for each component. The results are also shown below.

Question 1. In Stage 1, is there a significant, repeatable difference between the high and low levels?

Question 2. In Stage 2, identify the important and unimportant factors. Are there significant interaction effects?

Question 3. To what extent should the tolerances on the important factors be reduced?

Question 4. To what extent should the tolerances of the unimportant factors be opened up?

These are the answers to the exercise on variables search:

Question 1. The high and low median values are 738 and 1050. So $D = 312; \bar{d} = \dfrac{17 + 29}{2} = 23$. So $D{:}\bar{d}$ is much greater

Table 9-2. Variables search for engine control module.

FACTOR DESCRIPTION		FACTOR NOMINAL VALUE	FACTOR TOLERANCE	FACTOR LEVELS	
				HIGH (H)	LOW (L)
A.	RESISTOR: R85	0.68 OHMS	± 5%	0.68 OHMS	0.65 OHMS
B.	POWER SUPPLY VOLTAGE : V_{CC}	5.0 VOLTS	± 5%	5.0 VOLTS	4.75 VOLTS
C.	RESISTOR: R77	100 OHMS	± 1%	100 OHMS	99 OHMS
D.	RESISTOR: R75	787 OHMS	± 1%	787 OHMS	729 OHMS
E.	XSISTOR: Q8 SATURATION VOLTAGE	75 M.V.	150 M.V. MAX	75 M.V.	150 M.V.
F.	RESISTOR: R79	43 OHMS	± 5%	43 OHMS	40.85 OHMS
G.	INTEGRATED CIRCUIT: IC4	0 M.V.	± 8 M.V.	0 M.V.	-8 M.V.
	OFF-SET VOLTAGE				

STAGE 1	ALL FACTORS AT HIGH LEVELS	ALL FACTORS AT LOW LEVELS
	742 MA	1053 MA
	738 MA	1050 MA
	725 MA	1024 MA

STAGE 2	TEST NO.	COMBINATION	RESULTS (MA)	CONCLUSIONS
	1	$A_L R_H$	768	
	2	$A_H R_L$	1020	
	3	$B_L R_H$	704	
	4	$B_H R_L$	1051	
	5	$C_L R_H$	733	
	6	$C_H R_L$	1028	
	7	$D_L R_H$	745	
	8	$D_H R_L$	1018	
	9	$E_L R_H$	726	
	10	$E_H R_L$	1022	
	11	$F_L R_H$	733	
	12	$F_H R_L$	1020	
	13	$G_L R_H$	1031	
	14	$G_H R_L$	718	

than the required 1.25:1 difference and all three high levels outrank all three low levels. Hence there is a significant, repeatable difference between the best and worst levels.

Question 2. The control limits are: $M \pm 2.776 \, (\overline{d}/1.81) = M \pm 35.28$. So control limits (high side) are: $738 \pm 35.28 = 702.72$ to 773.28. Control limits (low side) are: $1050 \pm 35.28 = 1014.72$ to 1085.28. Based on these control limits, all factors A through F are unimportant, as are their associated interaction effects. The only important factor is G, the *IC* offset voltage. It is not only the Red X; it is a super Red X! It overshadows all the other factors put together. In fact, in this example, a capping run was unnecessary.

Questions 3 and 4. The answers to Questions 3 and 4 require further experimentation. In this actual case study (where the original Stage 1 and Stage 2 experiments were performed by a technician and completed in just two days), the *IC* offset voltage tolerance was cut in half to ± 4 M.V. In negotiations with the semiconductor supplier, he was encouraged to reduce his process variability, using DOE. The tolerances for the two ± 1 percent resistors were opened up to ± 5 percent and the costs reduced on their procurement. The tolerances for the four remaining components were not changed, mainly because there was no price advantage for the larger tolerances. *The total savings from quality improvement (defects down to zero) and procurement cost reductions amounted to $450,000 in the first year alone.*

10

Full Factorials: Ideal for Quantifying Interaction Effects

In full factorial experiments, the *objectives* are to:

- Pinpoint the most important variables—Red X, Pink X—following the homing-in, clue-generating techniques of multi-vari charts, components search, or paired comparisons
- Separate and quantify the main and interaction effects of the important variables
- Start the process of opening up tolerances on the unimportant variables

These objectives are similar to those for variables search. The main difference is that full factorials are used to investigate four or fewer variables, whereas in variables search the number is five or more. In attempting to identify the causes of variation, engineers sometimes cannot think of more than four causes. Alternatively, previous homing-in techniques may have reduced such causes to four or less. As a result, the full factorial technique is still a useful workhorse in DOE.

Principle

The power in full factorials is that every one of the four (or fewer) chosen variables is tested with all levels (generally two) of every other variable. Thus all possible combinations of factors and levels are tested, allowing for the systematic separation and quantification of all main effects, as well as all interaction effects—including two-factor interactions, three-factor interactions, and a four-factor interaction.

In full factorials, an investigation involving two factors and two levels is called a 2^2 factorial. An investigation involving three factors and two levels is called a 2^3 factorial. And an investigation involving four factors and two levels is called a 2^4 factorial. In this chapter, a 2^4 full factorial will be explained, because 2^2 and 2^3 factorials are simpler versions of the 2^4 factorial.

With four factors, each with two levels, there are 2^4 or sixteen combinations; hence sixteen experiments are required. In order to overcome residual error inherent in all experimentation, these sixteen experiments should be repeated (or replicated), making a total of thirty-two experiments. (A technique using end counts and overlaps can reduce the number of experiments to sixteen but is not discussed here in the interests of brevity.)

The sample size in each combination of factors (called cells) needs be no more than one to five for variables data but must be large enough in attribute data to be able to distinguish one cell output from another. As an example, if the objective is to detect a 5 percent problem and reduce it, the sample size in each cell would have to be increased to one hundred units in order to differentiate between various percent defectives in each cell. A better way to keep the quantity down would, of course, be to first resort to the technique of paired comparisons. From the strong clues thus provided, the levels of the variables fitting those clues will cause a clear difference in the degree of the defectiveness occurring in the small samples.

Another way to reduce the sample size for attribute-type defects is to quantify the severity of the defect on a numerical scale from, say, 1 to 10, with 10 being the most severe defect and 1 being the least severe defect. The product of the number of defects and their severity increases the defect score so that defect totals between levels can be differentiated with much smaller sample sizes.

Finally, the sequence of testing should not be done in a methodical, predictable manner, *but in a random order*. This allows numerous causes not included in the experiment an equal opportunity of entering or leaving the experiment. The random order of testing can be determined through a random number table, described in most texts on statistics and quality control. For instance, if the sixteen combinations or cells are labeled sequentially and a table of random numbers selects sixteen random numbers as shown below, the sequence of testing would follow the random numbers from low to high as follows:

Cell No.:	1	2	3	4	5	6	7	8	9	10	11	12	13	14	15	16
Random Nos.:	38	68	83	24	86	59	40	47	20	60	43	85	25	96	93	45
Testing Sequence:	4	11	12	2	14	9	5	8	1	10	6	13	3	16	15	7

Procedure (for a 2⁴ Factorial)

1. Select the four factors to be investigated, based on previous homing-in experiments (better) and/or engineering judgment (less effective). Designate them A, B, C, and D.

2. Determine two levels for each factor. The first level, labeled $(-)$, is usually, but not necessarily, the current level for that factor. The second level, labeled $(+)$, is assumed to produce better results, but, again, not necessarily so. A practical alternative is to measure the actual range of the factor used in the shop every day when many good and some not-so-good parts are made, calling that range $(+)$ to $(-)$.

3. Draw up a matrix (see Table 10-1) showing the sixteen combinations by which each factor is tested with each level of every other factor.
4. Randomize the sequence of testing each combination (or cell).
5. Run an experiment with each combination in the sequence indicated by the random order table and record the output in each cell.

Table 10-1.   Full factorials: wave solder case study.

Product EEC IV - Model 2201
CAL No. New Machine Electrovert 337-12

A (FLUX)

	A- (A19)		A+ (880)		
	SPEED: B- 4 ft/min.	SPEED: B+ 6 ft/min.	B-	B+	
PRE-HEAT 160°F **D-** (ANGLE 5° **C-**)	[1] - - - - 21 (19) 17	[3] - + - - 14 (15) 16	[2] + - - - 104 (106) 112	[4] + + - - 8 (8) 8	▶150
PRE-HEAT 220°F **D+**	[9] - - - + 17 (16) 15	[11] - + - + 64 (61) 58	[10] + - - + 1 (1) 1	[12] + + - + 0 (0) 0	▶78
D- (ANGLE 7° **C+**)	[5] - - + - 4 (4) 4	[7] - + + - 43 (45) 47	[6] + - + - 44 (41) 38	[8] + + + - 3 (3) 3	▶93
D+	[13] - - + + 32 (33) 34	[15] - + + + 14 (13) 12	[14] + - + + 10 (10) 10	[16] + + + + 0 (0) 0	▶56
	▼72	▼134	▼160	▼11	

4 Factor 2-Level Matrix

A- = 72 + 134 = 206
A+ = 160 + 11 = 171   A- Is Worse Than A+ By 35 Defects.*

B- = 72 + 160 = 232
B+ = 134 + 11 = 145   B- Is Worse Than B+ By 87 Defects.

C- = 150 + 78 = 228
C+ = 93 + 56 = 149   C- Is Worse Than C+ By 79 Defects.

D- = 150 + 93 = 243
D+ = 78 + 56 = 134   D- Is Worse Than D+ By 109 Defects.

(-) A19 FLUX (+) (880)
(-) 4' SPEED (+) 6'
(-) 5° ANGLE (+) 7°
(-) 160° PRE-HEAT (+) 220°

*These numbers for defect differences are for totals. They could be divided by 8 to obtain differences between the average of each level, a number less dependent upon the number of tests run.

6. Repeat Steps 4 and 5 using *another* random order for the second test sequences.
7. Calculate the average of the two readings in each cell.
8. For the thirty-two sets of readings, add all* the average readings in those cells where A is $(-)$ and all the average cell readings where A is $(+)$. The difference between $A(-)$ and $A(+)$ is due to factor A alone, because all other factors—B, C, and D—balance one another, i.e., have added, or subtracted, a constant to or from both levels, thereby not changing the original difference! Similarly, add all the average cell readings where B is $(-)$ and where B is $(+)$. The difference is due to factor B alone. In like manner, calculate the difference between the $C(-)$ and $C(+)$ average readings and the $D(-)$ and $D(+)$ average readings.
9. Construct an analysis of variance (ANOVA) table. The procedure is explained in detail, using the following case study.

Full Factorials: The Wave Solder Case Study

The purpose of a wave solder process is to solder electronic components to a printed circuit (pc) board. Prior to this process, components are machine-inserted onto a pc board. The assembly is then put on a belt conveyor and passed, first, through a preheat chamber and next given an application of flux, a chemical cleaning agent that removes oxides from the component and pc board leads. Finally, the assembly passes over a fountain (or wave) of molten solder at a given angle of incline at a predetermined temperature and at a predeter-

---

*The novice user of full factorials is tempted to select a single combination (cell) of factors that appears to produce the best output. This is a suboptimal solution. It ignores valuable data in the remaining fifteen cells. By looking at eight cells where a factor is $(-)$ and eight where it is $(+)$ we get a magnifying effect that permits a better determination of the appropriate level for each factor and the relationships between main effects and interaction effects.

mined speed to effect solder connections between the components and the board.

For many years, defect rates of 3 percent of the total number of connections had been tolerated as the best the process could achieve. In more modern measurements, this defect rate translates to 30,000 parts per million (ppm). A quality improvement team was able to reduce the defect rate to 1 percent, or 10,000 ppm, by redesigning the pc boards and improving solderability on the pc boards and component leads.

The team felt that the remaining improvements had to come from the wave solder process. Multi-vari studies indicated large variations within the board, rather than board-to-board or time-to-time variations. Four possible causes were identified, requiring a full factorial 2^4 experiment. The target was to reduce the defect rate from 10,000 ppm to 200 ppm.

Four factors and two levels for each factor were selected.

		Levels	
Letter	Factor	(−)*	(+)
A	Flux	A 19	A 880
B	Belt speed	4 ft/min	6 ft/min
C	Angle of incline	5°	7°
D	Preheat temperature	160°F	220°F

*The (−) levels represented current levels. The results of the experiments are shown in Table 10-1.

Procedure for Constructing an ANOVA Table

An analysis of variance (ANOVA) table was constructed, as shown in Table 10-2. The procedure is as follows:

1. In the "cell group" column, enter the cell numbers from Table 10-1.

Table 10-2. Full factorials: wave solder—ANOVA table.

Cell Group	Factors				2 Factors Interactions						3 Factors Interactions				4 Factors Interaction	Output
	A	B	C	D	AB	AC	BC	AD	BD	CD	ABC	ABD	ACD	BCD	ABCD	
1	-	-	-	-	+	+	+	+	+	+	-	-	-	-	+	19
2	+	-	-	-	-	-	+	-	+	+	+	+	+	-	-	108
3	-	+	-	-	-	+	-	+	-	+	+	+	-	+	-	15
4	+	+	-	-	+	-	-	-	-	+	-	-	+	+	+	8
5	-	-	+	-	+	-	-	+	+	-	+	-	+	+	-	4
6	+	-	+	-	-	+	-	-	+	-	-	+	-	+	+	41
7	-	+	+	-	-	-	+	+	-	-	-	+	+	-	+	45
8	+	+	+	-	+	+	+	-	-	-	+	-	-	-	-	3
9	-	-	-	+	+	+	+	-	-	-	-	+	+	+	-	16
10	+	-	-	+	-	-	+	+	-	-	+	-	-	+	+	1
11	-	+	-	+	-	+	-	-	+	-	+	-	+	-	+	61
12	+	+	-	+	+	-	-	+	+	-	-	+	-	-	-	0
13	-	-	+	+	+	-	-	-	-	+	+	+	-	-	+	33
14	+	-	+	+	-	+	-	+	-	+	-	-	+	-	-	10
15	-	+	+	+	-	+	+	-	+	+	-	-	-	+	-	13
16	+	+	+	+	+	+	+	+	+	+	+	+	+	+	+	0
Main & Interaction Contribution	-35	-87	-79	-109	-211	-47	+33	-189	+115	+35	+73	+139	+127	-181	+39	

RED X (FLUX+SPEED) ◀ (AB) PINK X (FLUX+PRE-HEAT) ◀ (AD)

THE (-) SIGN IN THE FACTOR A COLUMN IN THE LAST ROW INDICATES THAT A- IS WORSE THAN A+ BY 35 DEFECTS. SIMILAR SIGNS IN THE OTHER MAIN AND INTERACTION FACTORS INDICATES WHETHER THE (-) LEVEL OR (+) LEVEL IS WORSE.

2. In the "factors" column, enter the appropriate $(-)$ and $(+)$ signs for factors A, B, C, and D in cell 1. Here A, B, C, and D are all $(-)$. The $(-)$ and $(+)$ signs merely indicate the levels of the factors used. Similarly, enter the appropriate $(-)$ and $(+)$ signs for A, B, C, and D in the remaining fifteen cells.

3. In the "output" column, enter the average of the outputs recorded in each cell from Table 10-1.

4. In the two "factor interactions" columns, multiply, *algebraically*, the signs of A and B in cell 1 and record the sign of the product in the AB column. Here, because A and B are both $(-)$, the product sign for AB is $(+)$. Similarly, determine the algebraic products of A and C, B and C, etc., and record them in the appropriate two-factor interaction column.

5. Repeat the algebraic multiplications of A, B, and C; A, B, and D; etc., up to A, B, C, and D, and record the signs in the appropriate three-factor or four-factor interaction column.

6. Repeat Steps 4 and 5 for all remaining fifteen cells.

7. In column A, add all the outputs where A is $(-)$ and add all the outputs where A is $(+)$. Note the difference between these two sums in the last row labeled "main and interaction effects contribution." Place a $(-)$ sign ahead of this entry if the $A(-)$ sum is worse than the $A(+)$ sum, or a $(+)$ sign if the reverse is the case.

8. Similarly, add all the $(+)$ and $(-)$ outputs for each column B, C, and D, AB through CD, ABC through BCD, and $ABCD$ and note the difference in the last row, as in Step 7.

9. The last row now displays, in precise quantified form, the contribution of each main factor as well as each two-factor, three-factor, and four-factor interaction to the total variation.

Table 10-2 can now be interpreted as follows: The Red X is the interaction effect between A and B, i.e., between the flux and the belt speed. The Pink X is the interaction effect between A and D, i.e., between the flux and preheat temperature. The main effects of A, B, C, and D are relatively small compared to the interaction effects.

The last step is to plot the major interaction effects. The procedure is as follows:

1. For the BC interaction, observe the B and C columns jointly. Add all the outputs of those cells where both B and C are $(-)$. Add all the outputs where B is $(-)$ and C is $(+)$. Add the outputs where B is $(+)$ and C is $(-)$. Add the outputs where B is $(+)$ and C is $(+)$.

2. Repeat the procedure for the AD and BD interactions. For the sake of brevity, only a few interactions are considered here. The results are shown in the graph, Figure 10-1. All three graphs show the presence of strong interactions because of nonparallel responses.

3. From the AB interaction and the AD interaction, the best results (lowest defects) occur when A is $(+)$. This is confirmed in the last row of Table 10-2, where $A(-)$ is worse than $A(+)$ by 35 defects.

4. From the AB interaction, the best results (lowest defects) occur when B is $(+)$. This is confirmed in the last row of Table 10-2, where $B(-)$ is worse than $B(+)$ by 87 defects.

5. In the BD interaction, the best results appear to be $B(-)$ and $D(+)$. Yet the $D(+)$ slope is much less steep than the $D(-)$ slope. In such cases, the lower slope, i.e., $D(+)$, should be chosen. The reason is that if the preferred belt speed, $B(+)$, of 6 ft/min should "wander" toward $B(-)$, or 4 ft/min in production, and preheat temperature is held at the $D(-)$ level of 160°F, the defect level would increase rapidly, traveling along the $D(-)$ line. Hence $D(+)$ would be the *safer* level to use. This is further confirmed in the last row of Table 10-2, where $D(-)$ is worse than $D(+)$ by 109 defects.

Conclusion

The 2^4 factorial clearly showed that the best levels of the four factors were $A(+)$, $B(+)$, $C(+)$, and $D(+)$—in other

Figure 10-1. Interaction graph.

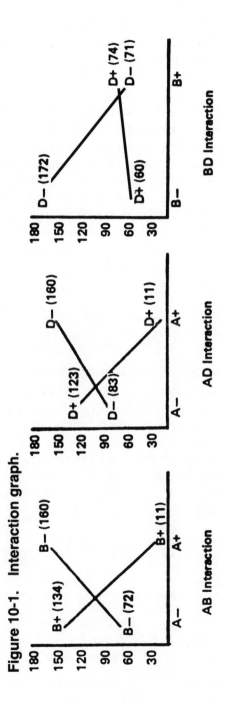

words, the use of the *A* 880 flux, the belt speed of 6 ft/min, an incline angle of 7°, and a preheat temperature of 220°F. A capping run (confirmation experiment) on seventeen boards produced three defects. With 800 connections per board, the defect rate dropped to 220 ppm. This represented a 45:1 quality improvement. When twelve other wave solder processes were similarly modified, twenty touch-up operators and an equivalent number of inspectors were eliminated for a yearly savings of $750,000! These are the kinds of spectacular results needed to solve problems. We must be totally discontented with 10 percent, 50 percent, or even 100 percent improvements. (Incidentally, neither the classical DOE fractional factorials nor the Taguchi methods could give comparable results.)

Practice Exercise on Full Factorials: The Drilling Operation

In the cross-drilling of two holes, 9/64″ diameter, through both walls of a piece part, a heavy exit burr and large hanging flags were present on over 50 percent of the parts. All shipments to date had been rejected by the customer, even after each part was blown out with high-pressure air. A 2^4 full factorial experiment was designed to optimize the parameters that could eliminate burrs and flags. Four machine parameters were selected with two levels for each factor. The $(-)$ levels represented current production.

	Levels	
Factor	*(−)*	*(+)*
A. Spindle speed (rpm)	2,850	5,000
B. Drill type	GT 100	Guhring Gold
C. Drill feed (in/rev)	0.001	0.003
D. Coolant type	Water-soluble mist	Cutting oil

Output. The parts were graded for severity on a numerical scale of 0 to 4.

	Scale
Minimal burr—nondefective	S0
Slight raised burr—higher than minimum	S1
Raised burr plus one hanging flag, easily broken off	S2
Raised burr plus two or more flags	S3
Excessive hanging burr and multiple flags	S4

The defect score in each cell was the number of each type of defect multiplied by the above scale.

Experiment. One hundred pieces were run in each cell combination. The sequence was randomized. A new drill was used in each experiment to eliminate the effect of tool wear. The factorial matrix and the ANOVA table are shown in Tables 10-3 and 10-4.

Question 1. Were one hundred pieces necessary for each cell?

Question 2. What were the benefits of grading the defects on a 0 to 4 scale?

Question 3. Based on the results of a single cell, what are the best levels to use? Why is this a poor conclusion?

Question 4. From the ANOVA table, which are the Red X and Pink X factors?

Question 5. What are the optimum levels to use for each factor?

Question 6. Does the graphical plot for interactions confirm these choices?

These are the answers to the exercise question on full factorials.

Question 1. If the defect rate had been small, 5 percent or less, one hundred pieces for each cell would have been justi-

Table 10-3. Full factorials: drill experiment—factorial matrix.

C DRILL FEED		SPINDLE SPEED A (-) : 2850 R.P.M.		A (+) : 5000 R.P.M.	
		* B(-) : GT 100	B+ : GUHRING GOLD	B (-) : GT 100	B(+) : GUHRING GOLD
C(-) 0.001	D(-) MIST	[1] [9] S1 : 37 S2 : 42 S3 : 13 S4 : 2 TOT: (168)	[2] [3] S1 : 9 S2 : 26 S3 : 54 S4 : 7 TOT: (251)	[3] [14] S1 : 42 S2 : 35 S3 : 3 TOT: (121)	[4] [5] S1 : 18 S2 : 30 S3 : 50 TOT: (228)
	D(+) OIL	[5] [11] S1 : 49 S2 : 41 S3 : 1 S4 : 2 TOT: (142)	[6] [10] S1 : 1 S3 : 1 S4 : 98 TOT: (396)	[7] [7] S1 : 34 S2 : 42 S3 : 6 S4 : 1 TOT: (140)	[8] [6] S1 : 3 S2 : 7 S3 : 46 S4 : 44 TOT: (331)
C(+) 0.003	D(-) MIST	[9] [8] S1 : 50 S2 : 43 S3 : 7 TOT: (157)	[10] [13] S1 : 15 S2 : 35 S3 : 45 S4 : 4 TOT: (236)	[11] [12] S1 : 53 S2 : 17 S3 : 3 S4 : 0 TOT: (96)	[12] [15] S1 : 62 S2 : 30 S3 : 2 TOT: (128)
	D(+) OIL	[13] [2] S1 : 22 S2 : 7 TOT: (36)	[14] [16] S1 : 35 S2 : 49 S3 : 10 S4 : 1 TOT: (167)	[15] [4] S1 : 5 S2 : 1 TOT: (7)	[16] [1] S1 : 11 TOT: (11)

QUESTION 1:	Were 100 pieces necessary for each cell?
QUESTION 2:	What were the benefits of grading the defects on a 0 - 4 scale?
QUESTION 3:	Based on the results of a single cell, what are the best levels to use ? Why is this a poor conclusion?
QUESTION 4:	From the ANOVA tables (next page), which are the Red X & Pink X factors?
QUESTION 5:	What are the optimum levels to use for each factor?
QUESTION 6:	Does the graphical plot for interactions confirm these choices?

*The first square in each cell corner represents the cell number. The second square in each cell represents the run sequence.

fied. With a defect rate of over 50 percent, a much smaller sample, say twenty units, would have been sufficient.

Question 2. There were two benefits to grading: (1) The defect scale was magnified. Hence differences between cells were also magnified. In fact, with the magnified scale, the sample size per cell could have been further reduced, say to ten. (2) If a particular type of defect had to be separated, e.g., burrs alone or flags alone, the matrix could easily have separated these two output categories.

Question 3. Based on a single cell, the best levels would be $A(+)$, $B(-)$, $C(+)$, $D(+)$. As it turned out eventually, this

Table 10-4. Full factorials: drill experiment—ANOVA table.

Cell Group	Factors				2 Factors Interactions						3 Factors Interactions				4 Factors Interaction	
	A	B	C	D	AB	AC	BC	AD	BD	CD	ABC	ABD	ACD	BCD	ABCD	Output
1	-	-	-	-	+	+	+	+	+	+	-	-	-	-	+	168
2	-	+	-	-	-	+	+	-	-	+	+	+	-	+	-	251
3	+	-	-	-	-	-	-	+	+	+	+	+	+	-	-	121
4	+	+	-	-	+	-	-	-	-	+	-	-	+	+	+	228
5	-	-	-	+	+	+	+	-	+	-	-	+	+	+	-	142
6	-	+	-	+	-	+	-	-	+	-	+	-	+	-	+	396
7	+	-	-	+	-	-	+	+	-	-	+	-	-	+	+	140
8	+	+	-	+	+	-	+	-	+	-	-	+	-	-	-	331
9	-	-	+	-	+	-	+	-	+	-	+	-	+	+	-	157
10	-	+	+	-	-	-	+	+	-	-	-	+	+	-	+	236
11	+	-	+	-	-	+	-	-	+	-	-	+	-	+	+	96
12	+	+	+	-	+	+	-	+	-	-	+	-	-	-	-	128
13	-	-	+	+	-	-	-	-	-	+	+	+	-	-	+	36
14	-	+	+	+	-	-	-	+	+	+	-	-	-	+	-	167
15	+	-	+	+	-	+	+	-	-	+	-	-	+	-	-	7
16	+	+	+	+	+	+	+	+	+	+	+	+	+	+	+	11
Main & Interaction Contribution	-491	+881	-939	-155	-213	-217	-13	-389	+279	-637	-135	-167	-19	-231	+7	

2 Factor Interactions

was the best combination. Nevertheless, a full ANOVA exercise is necessary so that the very useful data contained in the remaining fifteen cells are not thrown away.

Question 4. From the last row of the ANOVA table, the factor with the highest reading is C. Its best level should be $C(+)$. The next highest factor is B. Its best level should be $B(-)$.

Question 5. The optimum levels, based on the readings and signs in the last row of the ANOVA table, are $A(+)$, $B(-)$, $C(+)$, $D(+)$.

Question 6. The graphical plot can be interpreted as follows: In the CD interaction, $C(+)$, $D(+)$ gives the lowest defects. Hence those are the right levels for C and D, even though the $D(-)$ slope is gentler than the $D(+)$ slope. The physical rationale is that, in production, there is no danger of the coolant "wandering" to another type. Similarly in the BC

interaction, the $C(+)$, $B(-)$ combination gives the lowest defects and the lowest slope. In the BD interaction, the $B(-)$, $D(+)$ combination gives the lowest defects and $D(+)$ is chosen for the same reason as in the CD interaction. In the AC interaction, the $A(+)$, $C(+)$ combination gives the lowest defects and the two slopes are about equal.

Conclusion

The results were contrary to the engineering expectations, where the lower drill feed rate was thought to be better. With the combination of higher drill feed (Red X), the Guhring Gold drill type (Pink X), the higher spindle speed, and the cutting oil, the defect rate was reduced to *zero!*

Although these examples of full factorial designs showed how to get statistical estimates of the magnitude of each interaction and each main effect, a remaining question always has to be: Is the observed difference between the $(+)$ and the $(-)$ levels due merely to sampling chance, or is it more than chance can explain? The answer depends on how important it is that you don't reach a wrong conclusion, expressed as a probability number called statistical risk, say 0.05. Numerically, $1.00 - \text{risk} = \text{confidence}$, 0.95 in this example. Choosing such numbers before you run the tests, and how you calculate them to determine the number of tests to run, are the subjects of the next chapter. You will be introduced to rank order statistical analysis, which has not been appreciated by most professional problem solvers.

11

B vs. C: A Versatile, Universal Tool

In B vs. C analysis, the symbols B and C stand for two levels, $(+)$ and $(-)$, of a variable, or two processes or a pair of alternate methods or policies that need to be compared. C is, generally, the current (C) process, and B is, supposedly, a better (B) process. But they could also be two new processes. B vs. C is a nonparametric comparative experimentation, where no assumption of normality is necessary for either the B or C process distributions. The term *nonparametric* is a third form of data observation. In variables data, there is measurement, such as a dimension, where there can be a continuous scale of a vast number of different readings. In attributes data, there is only "good or bad," "accept or reject." In nonparametric data, there are no measurements as in variables, but only a ranking of units—from best to worst. The power of nonparametric ranking is that it takes only a comparison between extremely small sample sizes from the two processes—often just three from the B process and three from the C process—to ensure, with a very high degree of confidence, that one is better than the other.

Objective and Applications

In the design of experiments, B vs. C is generally used as a final validation of previous techniques, like multi-vari

117

charts and variables search, that had isolated the Red X. It can also be used at the very start of design of experiments, bypassing the other techniques, but only if engineering is sure that it has a better method or design. (Given the track record of some engineers in their ability to solve problems, this is a dangerous assumption!)

In addition, B vs. C is a versatile tool that goes beyond the arena of engineering and production into almost any field: white-collar work, social services, sales, human relations, etc. It is universal in scope, simple in implementation, low in costs, and powerful in statistical effectiveness.

Principle

Let us suppose that two processes—*C*, a current process, and *B*, a possibly better process—are to be compared. Normally, process capability studies would be run on them, with fifty to one hundred readings taken from each process. The results could be any of four frequency distributions shown in Figure 11-1. If the distributions of *B* and *C* are those in (1), it is obvious that there is no difference between *B* and *C*. This is called the null hypothesis. In (2), *B* is generally better than *C*, but there is overlap, with some *B* units worse than some C units. We can call this a Pink X condition. In (3), the worst *B* units are equal to or better than the best *C* units, a Red X condition. In (4), the worst *B* units are much better than the best *C* units, a super Red X condition.

This kind of determination, however, would require a minimum of fifty readings drawn from each process. *The power of* B *vs.* C *tests is that with just a few units—most frequently, three* B *units and three* C *units—we can determine, with a desired but practical level of risk of being wrong, whether the parent populations have distributions similar to (1), (3), or (4); (2) involves another kind of risk. These risks,* α *and* β, *respectively, are explained later in this chapter.*

The theory behind B vs. C is based on the formula for combinations (not permutations). If there are two *B* units and

Figure 11-1. Four distributions of *B* and *C* processes.

C = Current Process;   B = Better (?) Process

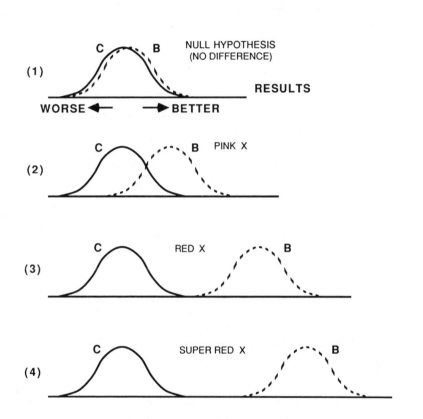

two *C* units, the possible ways they can be arranged in rank order (vertically) are:

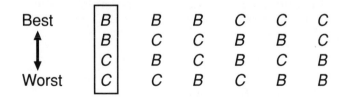

There are only six ways in which two *B*s and two *C*s can be ranked in any order. Of these, there is only one way out of six in which the two *B*s come out on top and the two *C*s are at the bottom. When that happens, the hypothesis of no difference is rejected. [Such a rejection is the objective of the B vs. C test. When we fail to reject (one of the other rankings occurs), we know that the (3) and (4) distributions in Figure 11-1 are not possible. When the populations don't overlap, the small samples from those populations can't overlap.] In other words, there is a one in six, or 16.7 percent, risk that if two *B*s come out on top and two *C*s are at the bottom, it is through chance alone. But we are *protected* (called statistical confidence). Similarly, if there are three *B* units and three *C* units, the number of ways they can be arranged in rank order (vertically) is:

	1	2	3	4	5	6	7	8	9	10	11	12	13	14	15	16	17	18	19	20
Best	B	B	B	B	B	B	B	B	B	B	C	C	C	C	C	C	C	C	C	C
	B	B	B	C	C	C	C	C	C	C	B	B	B	B	B	B	B	C	C	C
	B	C	C	B	C	B	B	C	C	C	B	B	B	C	C	C	B	B	B	C
	C	B	C	B	B	C	C	B	B	C	B	C	C	B	B	C	B	B	C	B
	C	C	C	C	B	B	C	B	C	C	B	C	B	C	B	B	C	B	B	B
Worst	C	C	B	C	C	C	B	C	B	B	C	C	B	C	B	B	C	B	B	B

There are twenty ways in which three *B*s and three *C*s can be ranked in any order. Of these, there is only one way in which all three *B*s can rank above all three *C*s by chance alone. Concluding that *B* is really better than *C* represents a one in twenty, or 5 percent, chance or risk. This is known as the α risk.

The formula for the number of possible combinations is

$$\frac{(n_B + n_C)!}{n_B! \, n_C!}$$

where n_B = no. of *B* samples

n_C = no. of *C* samples

! is a factorial. (As an example, 8! means: $8 \times 7 \times 6 \times 5 \times 4 \times 3 \times 2 \times 1$.)

The α risk, then, is:

$$\frac{1}{\text{tot. no. of combinations}} = \frac{1}{\dfrac{(nB + nC)!}{nB! \, nC!}} = \frac{nB! \, nC!}{(nB + nC)!}$$

In the case of 3 Bs and 3 Cs:

$$\text{the no. of combinations} = \frac{(3! + 3!)}{3! \, 3!} = \frac{6!}{3! \, 3!} =$$
$$\frac{6 \times 5 \times 4 \times 3 \times 2 \times 1}{3 \times 2 \times 1 \times 3 \times 2 \times 1} = 20$$

$$\alpha \text{ risk} = 1/20 = 0.05 \text{ or } 5\%$$

The matrix below relates two decisions an experimenter can make relative to the actual, but unknown, situation.

Decision Based on Experimental Analysis	Actual (Unknown) Situation	
	B is Better Than C	B is the Same as C
	Yes	No
B is Better Than C Yes	OK	Type I Error α Risk
B is the Same as C No	Type II Error β Risk	OK

If the experimenter decides that B is better than C (i.e., he is rejecting the null hypothesis [H_0] of B being the same as C) and B is truly better than C in the actual, but unknown, situation, the right decision was made. If, however, the actual situation contains no improvement, the experimenter will have committed a Type I error and its probability is the alpha (α) risk.

If the experimenter decides that B is the same as C (i.e., he is *not* rejecting the null hypothesis) and B is truly the same as C in the actual situation, the right decision was made. If, however, the actual situation has an improvement by an amount worth detecting (this is called the alternative hypothesis, H_1), the experimenter will have committed a Type II error, and its probability is the beta (β) risk.

The α risk, therefore, is defined as the risk of rejecting the null hypothesis, i.e., assuming improvement, when no improvement exists. The β risk is defined as the risk of accepting the null hypothesis, i.e., assuming that there is no improvement, when a desirable improvement does exist.

Table 11-1 is an important chart that enables the appropriate sample sizes to be selected for B vs. C tests, along with predesignated α and β risks. Dorian Shainin calls it his "superhuman table" because working with a consistent risk—even as large as 0.10—is several times better than any "expert" can do without this empirical aid.

Procedure

Step 1. Choose an Acceptable Level of α Risk

There are four choices of α risks in Table 11-1, ranging from 0.10 to 0.001, i.e., from 10 percent to 0.1 percent risks. (Because risk plus confidence equals 1, the confidence levels range from 0.90 to 0.999, i.e., from 90 percent to 99.9 percent.) The α risk choice must be made a priori, i.e., before the fact. In most industrial situations, companies properly use the "default" level of an 0.05 risk. The other three levels of risk are *moderate*: 0.10 (for R&D looking for smaller Red Xs); *critical*: 0.01 (where the Red X has to be stronger to be detectable), the setting used when human life and large losses of time and money may be involved; and *supercritical*: 0.001, where consequences such as food poisoning or disasters of the magnitude of Chernobyl and Bhopal are at issue.

Step 2. Decide on Sample Sizes for B and C Tests

Table 11-1 contains the sample sizes for B and C tests, once the appropriate α risk is selected. There are several

Table 11-1. B vs. C table for a one-tailed test (*B* better than *C*, not just different).

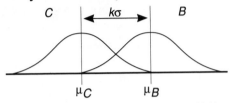

$$k = \frac{\mu_B - \mu_C}{\sigma_{Smaller}}$$

Desired Conf.	α Risk	Number of Randomized Samples B	Number of Randomized Samples C	Values of k (Desired Minimum): Assume $\sigma_B = \sigma_C$ β Risk 0.50	0.10	0.05	$\sigma_C = 1.5\sigma_B$, or $\sigma_B = 1.5\sigma$ β Risk 0.50	0.10	0.05
0.999	0.001	2	43	3.0	4.0	4.3	3.9	5.1	5.5
		3	16	2.5	3.6	3.9	3.2	4.5	5.0
Supercritical		4	10	2.3	3.4	3.8	2.9	4.3	4.8
		5	8	2.2	3.4	3.7	2.9	4.3	4.7
		6	6	2.2	3.3	3.7	2.8	4.2	4.7
0.99	0.01	2	13	2.3	3.4	3.8	3.0	4.4	4.8
		3	7	2.1	3.2	3.6	2.6	4.1	4.6
Critical		4	5	2.0	3.1	3.5	2.5	4.0	4.5
		5	4	2.0	3.1	3.5	2.5	4.0	4.5
0.95	0.05	1	19	2.5	3.6	3.9	3.2	4.6	5.0
		2	5	1.7	3.0	3.4	2.2	3.8	4.3
Important		3	3	1.6	2.9	3.3	2.0	3.7	4.2
		4	3	1.7	3.0	3.4	2.2	3.8	4.3
0.90	0.10	1	9	2.1	3.2	3.6	2.6	4.1	4.6
		2	3	1.4	2.7	3.2	1.8	3.5	4.0
Moderate		3	2	1.4	2.7	3.2	1.8	3.5	4.0

Consequences of a Wrong Decision

No Overlap of Ranks Is Permitted by This Test

Source: Copyright 1988 Shainin Consultants, Inc.

possible combinations. Because *C* is the current process, there are likely to be more *C* units available for testing than *B* units from a newer process.

However, a simple guideline for most comparative experiments in industry is to use an α risk of 5 percent (or a confidence of 95 percent) and then to select three B units and three C units. This gives one of the best balances between risk and the cost of experimentation.

Step 3. Randomize and Conduct the Tests

As in factorial experiments, randomizing the sequence of testing, say, three Bs and three Cs, is mandatory. Randomizing filters out the effects of environmental factors, human bias, time of day, and other variables, so that the test results can be correctly attributed to an assignable cause, namely, the variable(s) altered from C to B. It is tempting, in production, to run three Cs with the existing process and then switch over to the B process. But that would defeat randomization, and the results could be invalid.

Step 4. Rank Order the Results

Although ranking first requires measuring each B and C unit using a quantitative parameter, the ranking itself is qualitative, going only from best to worst.

Step 5. Decision Rule

Based on the ranking, there are two approaches to a decision:

1. *The no overlap technique.* This is more properly referred to as a *no overlap end count.* In any ordered ranking of samples, the end count is that collection of either B or C samples that is unpolluted by samples from the other group. As an example, if there were three Bs and four Cs and the ranking were as follows,

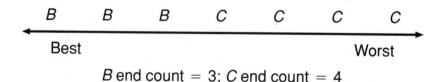

B	B	B	C	C	C	C

Best   Worst

B end count = 3; C end count = 4

There is no overlap: The B end count is 3, the C end count is 4, and the total end count is 7.

In the no overlap end count technique, no overlap of Bs and Cs is allowed. In the above case, the three Bs outrank the four Cs and so B is judged to be a better process, with 95 percent confidence (or with an α risk of 5 percent of assuming improvement when there could be no improvement). If only one or two Bs outrank the Cs, i.e., if there is overlap between the B and C rankings, B is not considered better than C and the decision will be not to make the change.

2. *The overlap end count technique.* In several industrial situations, it may be preferable to allow some overlap and still keep the risk of wrong decisions very low. In this case, the *overlap end count technique* will be used. As an example, the ranking of five Bs and five Cs is as follows:

B	B	B	C	B	B	C	C	C	C

Best ← → Worst

B end count = 3; *C* end count = 4; total end count = 7

Here, overlap exists. If overlap is to be allowed, the procedure (Step 2) changes slightly. The sample sizes for B and C are larger, generally ten or more for each, and equal. If they are unequal, the sample size for B, i.e., n_B, could be either smaller or larger than for C, i.e., n_C. But the ratio of $n_B:n_C$ should be no more than 3:4. The larger sample sizes make the overlap technique slightly more expensive than the no overlap technique, but there is a resultant improvement in representing the population.

If n_B is equal to n_C or no further away than a 3:4 ratio, B is better than C when:

α Risk	End Count Is $\geq$*
0.10	6
0.05	7
0.01	10
0.001	13

*John W. Tukey, "A Quick, Compact Two Sample Test to Duckworth's Specifications," *Technometrics* 1, No. 1 (February 1959).

Step 6. Separate the Means: The β Risk

It might not be enough, at the start of B vs. C testing, to determine only whether B is better than or the same as C (α risk). It may be economically and/or technically useful to determine, a priori again, the desired *magnitude* of the real improvement. The β risk is associated with this magnitude—separation of the mean (average) of B and the mean of C. The separation, or delta (Δ) distance, is measured in $k\sigma_C$ units, where k is a stipulated number selected by the experimenter before testing begins and σ_C is the standard deviation of the C process. (The B process may have too few units to determine an accurate σ_B.) Table 11-1 shows the k values for β risks of 0.5, 0.1, and 0.05. As an example, if one enters Table 11-1 with an α risk of 0.05, with three Bs and three Cs chosen as sample sizes and the assumption that $\sigma_B = \sigma_C$, the indication is that for a β risk of 0.1, k should be 2.9. In other words, if the separation between the mean of B and C is at least $2.9\sigma_C$, then there is only a 0.1 (or 10 percent) probability that this improvement will go undetected. If there is larger improvement between the mean of B and C—$3.3\sigma_C$ or more—then there is only a 0.05 (5 percent) probability that such improvement will go undetected. The relationship between the separation of the B and C means and the associated β risks is summarized graphically in Figure 11-2. (Assume $\sigma_B = \sigma_C$.)

3 *B*s and 3 *C*s: α risk = 0.05

.50, 50 reference (k = 1.6) will be detected only half of the time.

(k = 2.9) will be detected 90 percent of the time.

(k = 3.3) will be detected 95 percent of the time.

Uses of B vs. C

Even if the B vs. C tests indicate that there is no difference between the two processes in terms of quality, the B

Figure 11-2. Three *B*s and *C*s: α risk = 0.05.

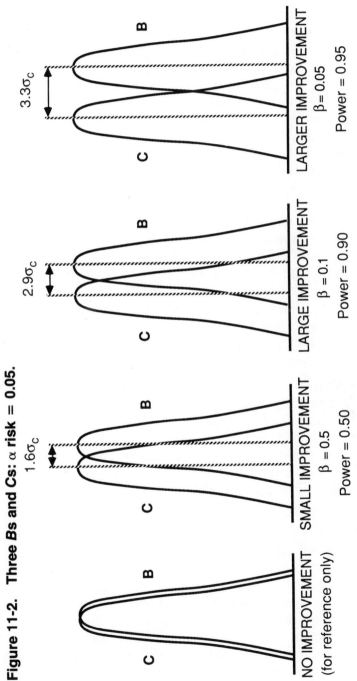

NO IMPROVEMENT
(for reference only)

SMALL IMPROVEMENT
β = 0.5
Power = 0.50

LARGE IMPROVEMENT
β = 0.1
Power = 0.90

LARGER IMPROVEMENT
β = 0.05
Power = 0.95

$1.6\sigma_c$

$2.9\sigma_c$

$3.3\sigma_c$

process can still be selected over the C process (or vice versa) if the B process is *less expensive* than the C process. (Of course, if the B process is worse than the C process in terms of quality, the switch to B should not be made.) Lowering costs is, sometimes, as valuable as a quality improvement.

As stated earlier, B vs. C is such a versatile tool that it can be used not only in engineering and manufacturing but in almost any field of human endeavor where quick and easy comparisons can be made. This includes marketing, sales, advertising, human relations, forecasting, etc.

As an example, if a car manufacturer wishes to determine which of two styling approaches, B or C, is better, a quick and easy test would be to pick three typical customers and ask them, independently and separately, to indicate their preference for the B or C styling. If all three customers chose B over C, there would be a high confidence that the B styling was better. If there was no clear separation of B over C, the two stylings would not be perceived as significantly different. When either an improvement or an economic gain (with no improvement) is an expectation, B vs. C tests can be used for:

- Evaluation of the effectiveness of design, process, and material changes
- Reliability evaluations
- Customer preferences
- Sales/marketing/service practices
- Sales promotions/advertising
- Human relations policies

Caution: B vs. C can be an amazingly effective small sample decision-making aid provided the user takes the time to understand the inference and time situations just described, and provided the value of *risk* desired, measured as how often in the long run the evaluator *could* be wrong, is understood. One can learn to use clue generators (multi-vari charts, paired comparisons, components search patterns, and the like) to select what B will represent, to be compared with C. Then sketches (3) and (4) of Figure 11-1 will exist, and one will make the correct decision from the test—that the Red X is confirmed—100 percent of the time.

B vs. C Case Study: The 64 K RAM

In the fabrication of a 64 K RAM (semiconductor), a B vs. C test was run to see if standard substrates (*C*) in a room atmosphere could be produced in a high-oxygen atmosphere (*B*) in order to improve yields. An electric parameter was chosen (not identified because of confidentiality). The α risk was chosen at 0.05 (5 percent) but the usual three *B*s and three *C*s were deemed to be an inadequate sample. Twelve *C* and thirteen *B* samples were selected and processed in random order. It was decided to use the overlap end count technique. The results were:

C (Standard Substrates: Room Atmosphere)
105.6, 102.5, 108.5, 114.6, 95.8, 88.3, 104.1, 100.5, 97.5, 114.9, 103.7, 100.0

B (High-Oxygen Substrates)
106.7, 101.2, 119.2, 108.6, 117.0, 109.4, 123.6, 117.2, 114.5, 123.2, 99.3, 110.4, 118.2

The results were ranked in descending order as follows:

B 123.6 ⎫
B 123.2 ⎪
B 119.2 ⎬ *B* end count = 6
B 118.2 ⎪
B 117.2 ⎪
B 117.0 ⎭
C 114.9, *C* 114.6, *B* 114.5, *B* 110.4, *B* 109.4, *B* 108.6, *C* 109.5, *B* 106.7, *C* 105.6, *C* 104.1, *C* 103.7, *C* 102.5, *B* 101.2, *C* 100.5, *C* 100.0, *B* 99.3
C 97.5
C 95.8   *C* end count = 3
C 88.3

Analysis. Total end count = 6 + 3 = 9. So the 6, 7, 10, 13 (John Tukey) rule is met, where for $\alpha = 0.05$, the total end count must be at least 7. Therefore B process is better than C process with 95 percent confidence.

Practice Exercise on B vs. C: The Tuning Coil

A process change on a tuning coil was expected to in-crease torque, measured in inch-ounces. It was decided to list four C samples (current process) and four B samples (new process). It was stated that the proposed change would only be put into effect if all B samples outranked all C samples (no overlap).

All tests were run in random order. The results were (in terms of inch-ounces):

$$B\ 4.1, 4.3, 3.7, 4.2$$
$$C\ 3.6, 3.8, 2.5, 3.1$$

Question 1. What is the B end count? What is the C end count? What is the total end count? If there is overlap, what is its count?

Question 2. Based on the decision rule chosen (no over-lap), what decision would be made about switching or not switching to the new process?

Question 3. If the decision rule chosen had been the overlap end count technique and an α risk of 0.05 had been selected, would the new process have been adopted?

These are the answers to the exercise on the uses of B vs. C:

Question 1. The ranking was as follows:

B (4.3), B (4.2), B (4.1), C (3.8), B (3.7), C (3.6), C (3.1), C (2.5)
Best   Worst

B end count = 3   Overlap = 2 C end count = 3

Question 2. Because the decision rule had been selected a priori as no overlap, the proposed change is *not* an improvement.

Question 3. With the overlap end count technique selected a priori, the 6, 7, 10, 13 rule says that for an α of 0.05, the total end count should be a minimum of 7. The ranking shows a total end count of 6. Hence the proposed change does not represent an improvement.

We can conclude that the above exercise shows the importance of selecting the α risk and the decision rule in advance of running the experiment. With an understanding of the logic of B vs. C, refer to Figure 11-1. Sketches (3) and (4), where the underlying populations do not overlap, could not produce finite samples that overlap. Sketch (2) can produce sample overlap. Now the reader can appreciate the role of the magnitude of the difference between the true but unknown population *means,* expressed as $k\sigma$. Table 11-1 displays on the right the desired (a priori) minimum k values for the selected values of β risk. The John Tukey end count figures, the 6, 7, 10, 13 rule, do not apply to $(1.00 - \beta) =$ the "power" (ability) of the test to detect an improvement of at least a desired amount.

12

Scatter Plots (Realistic Tolerance Parallelogram Plots): For Optimization and Establishing Realistic Tolerances

Ninety percent of technical people do not establish tolerances on input parameters—be they components in a product or process characteristics—correctly. The methods include pulling tolerances out of the air, asking a neighbor, boiler-plate figures, suppliers' catalog recommendations, worst case analysis, or—at best—computer simulations. Their effectiveness ranges from "hit and miss" to under-spec-ing to over-spec-ing, resulting in considerable economic loss.

The best way, as well as the simplest, easiest, and most cost-effective way, is to use a graphical method called scatter plots (or their formal, more precise name, realistic tolerance parallelogram plots).

In a DOE study, such as a variables search, let us say that the high level of a particular Red X variable gives the best results and its low level gives poor results. But how do we know that the high level of this Red X variable is truly the best level? Could a level slightly on one side or the other of this level give even better results? The purpose of a scatter plot is to fine-tune the high or good level of a Red X or Pink X variable pinpointed in a previous DOE study, and determine its very best (optimum) level, i.e., the design center, as well as the realistic tolerances of the variable to ensure zero defects.

Scatter plots (known formally as Realistic Tolerance Parallelogram Plots) represent a graphical technique in which thirty readings of a range of values of an independent variable are plotted, in a random time sequence, against the corresponding range of values of a dependent output. If there is a correlation between these two variables—a thin line or parallelogram—the independent variable is Red X, and its most appropriate target value and tolerance can be graphically determined. If there is little or no correlation, the independent variable is not important and its value and tolerance can be placed at much less conservative levels that are the most economical.

Application and Principle

Scatter plots are used primarily for relating the target and proper tolerance values for the few important input variables (X) to the output quality characteristic requirement (Y) perceived by the customer. The plot is not used for problem solving, because it shows association and not necessarily cause and effect. It follows multi-vari charts, variables search, full factorials, and B vs. C tests as the last tool to be used in the DOE arsenal. It is a substitute for more sophisticated techniques such as evolutionary optimization (EVOP). As with other DOE techniques, its appeal is its simplicity and its graphical, nonmathematical approach.

Scatter plot principles are best illustrated by the graphical sketches shown in Figure 12-1. Let us assume that the

Figure 12-1.   Various scatter diagrams.

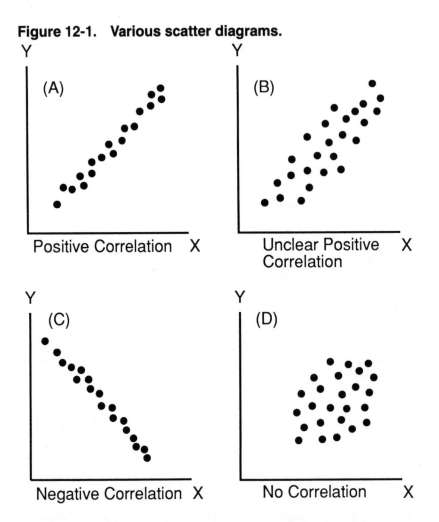

effect of an independent variable, X, upon a dependent variable, Y, is to be seen. An example would be the thickness of a membrane filter as X and the fluid flow rate through that filter as Y. A minimum of thirty filters are measured for thickness and for their individual, corresponding flow rates and the paired results plotted. If the plot is as shown in (A), there appears to be strong evidence of filter thickness directly affecting filter flow rate. As the thickness increases, the flow rate also increases proportionately. This is called a positive correlation. In (B), the correlation is not as strong. The thickness seems to produce a greater amount of different flow rates. In (C) there is also a strong correlation, but the slope is negative. It means that as the thickness increases, the flow rates decrease proportionately. This is called a negative correlation. Finally, in (D), there appears to be no correlation. For the same filter thickness, there are widely differing flow rates.

Figure 12-2 is a further interpretation of scatter plots. It shows three independent variables, X_2, X_6, and X_7, affecting a dependent output, Y. Which is the Red X, the variable that most controls variation in Y? The novice might say that it is X_7, because it has the greatest slope. But the slope is dependent on arbitrary scales for X_2, X_6, and X_7. If the scale for X_6 had been made finer, say, doubled, the slope would tilt downward to a flatter condition. *The Red X is the variable that has the lowest vertical scatter.* In Figure 12-2 it is X_6. One way to interpret vertical scatter is to draw a vertical line through the center of the ellipse that circumscribes the thirty plots. For a constant value of X it shows that Y has some variation, which, because X is constant, must be caused by all the other X variables. *Hence, vertical scatter is a measure of the total contribution to* Y *of all the variables added together, other than the particular* X. In Figure 12-2, X_6 has the lowest vertical scatter, followed by X_7 (a Pink X) and X_2 (a Pale Pink X).

Procedure for Determining Realistic Tolerances

1. Select the output (Y) to be met. Practically, the Red X, Pink X, etc., will have been pinpointed through the use of earlier DOE methods such as the multi-vari chart, variables search, and/or full factorials and confirmed with B vs. C tests.

2. Select a range of values for the Red X variable that is likely to fine-tune the output variable (Y). Run thirty such values of the Red X and note the corresponding Y values. Plot the results. If there is *tilt* in the graphics plot (the tilt need not be 45°, because the angle depends on the scale used for

Figure 12-2. Interpretation of vertical scatter.

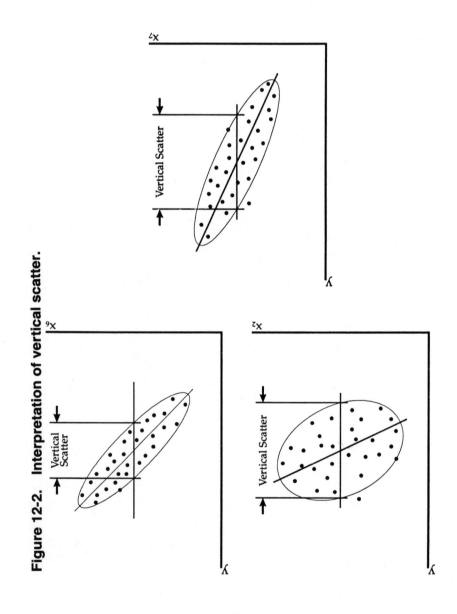

the Red X) and only a small vertical scatter, there is further validation of the Red X. (See Figure 12-3.) If there is no tilt, or the plot is a wide ellipse as in Figure 12-1 (D), the variable X is unimportant.

3. Draw a median line, called the line of regression, through the thirty plots. Draw two lines on each side of the median and parallel to it so as to contain all but one and a half of the thirty points. The vertical intercept through this parallelogram is the variation in Y due to all variables added together, other than the Red X. If this intercept is large (a fat parallelogram), the variable is a Pink X rather than a Red X.

4. If Y is a customer requirement, in terms of an upper specification limit, plot these points on the Y axis and draw two lines from them parallel to the X axis until the line from the upper specification limit intersects the upper boundary of the scatter and the line from the lower specification limit

Figure 12-3. Tolerance parallelogram (determining realistic tolerances).

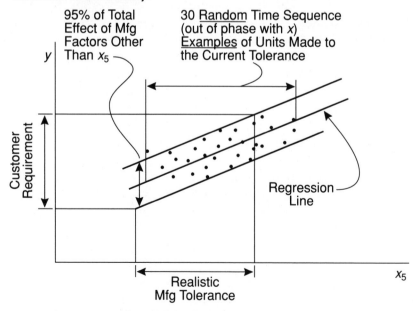

Source: Copyright 1988 Shainin Consultants, Inc.

intersects the lower boundary of the scatter. Drop two lines from these intersection points perpendicular to the X axis.

5. The horizontal intercept on the X axis between these two lines determines the maximum tolerances permitted for the Red X in order to ensure conformance to customer requirements. This would specify a minimum C_p of 1.0. Using precontrol rules, the horizontal intercept could be divided into four equal parts and only the middle half allowed as the preferred tolerance for the Red X. This would ensure a minimum C_p of 2. Further, the target value of the Red X variable should be at the center of the horizontal intercept.

6. These correct target values and tolerances for the Red X should be compared against existing values and tolerances and the necessary changes made to ensure zero defects and 100 percent yields.

Realistic Tolerances With Scatter Plots
Case Study

In the fabrication of an engine ignition amplifier, production was experiencing a fairly high reject rate in a critical parameter, off-time, which determines the amount of time (in milliseconds) that the ignition is turned off in a rapid cycle of on-and-off switching. Previous studies had identified the Red X and Pink X respectively as R_3 and R_4 resistors. Figure 12-4 plots the range of R_3 and R_4 values.

The results show that R_4 was correctly identified as the Pink X. Its correlation with the off-time output is clear, but weak. The parallelogram is fat and the vertical intercept is about 60 percent of the total output specification width of 1.2 milliseconds (from 6 to 4.8 ms). This means that 60 percent of the variation is caused by all factors other than R_4. However, the plot graphically shows that the original resistance of 110 K ohms $\pm$ 10 percent was wrong and was one of the causes of the high reject rate. The maximum range should be from 94 to 102 K ohms, with the center value of 98 K ohms. This would ensure a C_{pk} of 1.0. The optimum range should be from 96 to 100 K ohms (half the tolerance) to ensure a C_{pk} of 2.0.

Figure 12-4. Tolerance parallelogram case study: the ignition amplifier.

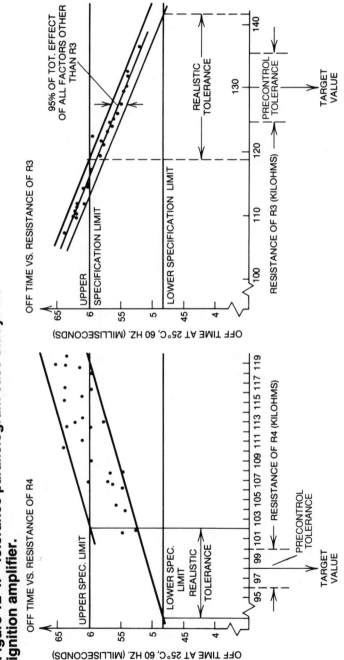

The R_3 plot clearly identifies resistor R_3 as the Red X, with a thin parallelogram. The vertical intercept is only about 16 percent of the total output specification width of 1.2 ms (from 6 to 4.8 ms). This means that only 16 percent of the variation is caused by all factors other than R_3. However, the plot graphically shows that the original resistance of 120 K ohms ± 10 percent was wrong, leading to the major cause of the high reject rate of the ignition amplifier. The graph shows that the maximum range allowed should be from 118.5 K to 141.5 K ohms, with the center at 130 K ohms. This would indicate a minimum C_{pk} of 1.0. The optimum range can now be determined by the C_{pk} desired. If a C_{pk} of 2.0 is sufficient, the range would be from 124 K to 135 K ohms. If a C_{pk} of 4.0 is required, the range would be from 127 K to 132 K ohms. The final ranges should be based upon the desirability of achieving these values, balanced by economics.

Practice Exercise on Scatter Plots:
The Digital Circuit

An output voltage in a digital circuit must be kept in the "on" or 1 condition to be considered acceptable. The "off" or 0 condition is considered unacceptable. Previous studies of the circuit had identified a 1,000 ohm resistor in the digital circuit as the Red X. Its tolerance was specified at ± 1 percent.

It was decided to check the validity of both the resistor value and its tolerance with a scatter plot shown here.

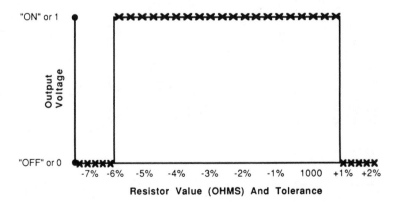

Question 1. Is 1,000 ohms the right value? If not, what should be the target valve for the resistor?

Question 2. Is the ± 1 percent tolerance right? If not, what should be the right resistor tolerance?

The answers follow:

Question 1. In this example, we are dealing with attributes—1: good and 0: bad. So there is no tilt in the plot. The resistor at exactly 1,000 ohms would give good results, but it is not centered. The center should be at a tolerance of 7%/2 = 3.5%, i.e., at 975 ohms.

Question 2. The tolerance could be opened up to ± 3.5 percent. However, that would only achieve a C_{pk} of 1.0. If the original tolerance of ± 1 percent is retained, the C_{pk} would be 3.5. In this example, if there is no great economic penalty in retaining a ± 1 percent tolerance, that would be optimum. If there is an economic penalty, the tolerance could be opened up to, say, ± 2 percent, but no more.

13

A Case Study Encompassing a Logical Sequence of the Seven DOE Tools

This chapter describes a comprehensive case study, using most of the seven DOE tools. It shows the linkage between these tools and the systematic approach used to achieve a quality breakthrough (down to zero defects) in the number of solder defects on a complex electronics circuit board. (The board name, the specific levels of the significant variables, and a few responses have been slightly altered in order to protect company confidentiality.)

Product:	EXO 5500 digital I/O panel (Each panel has five boards. Each board has one thousand solder joints.)
Process:	Wave soldering
Defect Level:	2,400 to 3,500 ppm Average: 2,970 ppm
Cost of Defects:	Inspection, scrap, rework, retest, assembly line and field failures: $8,900/month

Defect Modes:	80 percent solder shorts; 14 percent unsoldered connections; 6 percent pinholes, insufficient solder, etc.
Problem Duration:	Fourteen months
Problem-Solving Techniques to Date:	Traditional: process-tweaking, more frequent maintenance; brainstorming, cause and effect diagram

DOE Experiment 1: Multi-Vari Study

It was decided to conduct a multi-vari study first to determine the *family* of the Red X; that is, time-to-time, panel-to-panel, board-to-board, and within-board variations. Three panels, each containing five boards, were run at three time intervals: 9 A.M., 11 A.M., and 2 P.M.

Figure 13-1 shows the results of the multi-vari study in chart form.

Multi-Vari Chart Interpretations

Figure 13-1 indicates that the total defect count of 140 translates to a defect rate of 3,111 ppm (based on a total of 1,000 solder joints/board × 5 boards per panel × 3 panels/ time period × 3 time periods). This is slightly above the historical average of 2,970 ppm and therefore meets the empirical rule in multi-vari charts that at least 80 percent of the historical defect level must be captured during the multi-vari run.

- Figure 13-1A shows no significant variations from one time period to the next. The 9 A.M. time has the largest number of defects at 53 and the 11 A.M. time has the lowest number of defects at 40—a variation of 13 defects.
- Figure 13-1A also shows no significant variations be-

Figure 13-1.   Multi-vari chart on a wave soldering process.

(Total Defect Count: 140)

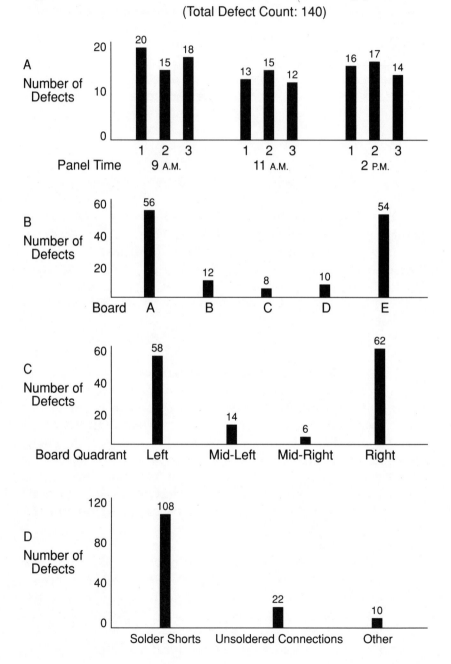

tween the three panels run consecutively at each time interval. The 9 A.M. time has the largest variation between the three panels (20 defects for panel 1 versus 15 defects for panel 2—a total panel-to-panel variation of 5).

- Figure 13-1B, by contrast, shows a very significant variation between the five boards and their location in the panel. Boards A and E, at the ends of the panel, show large defects, whereas boards B, C, and D in the middle show substantially reduced defects. The board-to-board variation is 46 defects.

- Figure 13-1C shows the most significant variation between the four quadrants within each board. The left and right quadrants—at each end of a board—display the largest number of defects, while the two middle quadrants have the least number of defects. The variation from quadrant to quadrant is 56 defects.

- Figure 13-1D displays the defects by type. The solder shorts account for the largest number of defects at 108, while the unsoldered connections and other defects (insufficient solder, pinholes, etc.) account for 22 and 10 respectively. This is similar to the historical profile.

The exact location of each solder defect was marked on a chart depicting the hole/component locations on a panel of five boards. (This is known as a concentration diagram or by its more popular name, a "measles" chart, not shown here.) The object is to pinpoint those hole and/or component locations with repetitive defects in order to determine further experiments and corrective actions. Each time period and each defect type is color-coded to facilitate the analysis.

Conclusions

1. Figure 13-1B showed that the outer boards in each panel had defect rates four times higher than those of the inner boards. This pointed to a paired comparisons

study of "good" versus "bad" boards among the several panels run.

2. Figure 13-1C showed that the left and right quadrants had defect rates four to five times higher than those of the middle quadrants. The measles chart revealed that the highest number of solder shorts (the number one type of defect) were in the edge connector region at the right end of each board. A second concentration of solder shorts in the measles chart was in the *IC* leads on the left end of each board. These solder shorts suggested that process parameters within the wave solder machine were the likely causes of the defects.

3. The unsoldered connections, though few in number, had repetitive rejects in the same two hole locations. Here again a paired comparisons study of "good" solder connections versus "bad" unsoldered connections in the same geographical area was in order.

DOE Experiment 2: Paired Comparisons

Experiment 2A

Four of the nine panels run in Experiment 1—the multi-vari study—were selected to compare the "good" inner boards in each panel versus the "bad" outer boards. The results are shown in Table 13-1. The multi-vari clue pointed to a possible warp of the panels going through the wave soldering process. The degree of warp was used as the output (that is, response parameter).

Conclusion

The paired comparisons study showed a repetitive difference in warp between the two inner boards and the two outer boards (the center of the middle board, C, was used as a reference), ranging from 0.15" for the inner boards up to almost 0.3" for the outer boards on four pairs of boards.

Table 13-1.   Paired comparisons of inner and outer boards.

Panel No.	Pair	Warp (From Panel Center to Center of Each Board)	
		Left Board	*Right Board*
1	Inner Boards	0.008"	0.010"
	Outer Boards	0.150"	0.170"
2	Inner Boards	0.010"	0.015"
	Outer Boards	0.210"	0.250"
3	Inner Boards	0.015"	0.012"
	Outer Boards	0.300"	0.260"
4	Inner Boards	0.013"	0.010"
	Outer Boards	0.190"	0.160"

Corrective Action

The excessive warp indicated that the panel fixturing could be inadequate and that the temperatures in the pre-heat zones could be too high. The panel fixtures were modified to ensure firmer panel anchoring and each preheat zone temperature was lowered by 10°F to lower the total amount of heat generated.

Experiment 2B

Another paired comparisons study (not shown) was made on four boards, where there were repetitive unsoldered connections in the same location on each board. These locations were compared against adjacent locations with perfect solder connections. Comparisons revealed no differences between the "good" and "bad" solder connections in terms of plating in the hole or the solder coat on the leads. However, the "bad" solder connections had a higher hole-to-lead diameter ratio than the "good" solder connections by factors ranging from 1.4:1.0 up to 1.7:1.0.

Corrective Action

It was determined that a uniform drill-bit size had been used to fabricate the printed circuit boards. As a result, those components with small lead diameters were more prone to unsoldered connections than the majority of components with larger lead diameters. Smaller drill-bit sizes were specified in the fabrication of the next batch of boards.

DOE Experiment 3: B vs. C

Next, a B vs. C experiment was conducted to determine the effectiveness of the corrective actions following Experiment 2.

C process: Current fixtures; current preheat zones; current drill-bit sizes in board fabrication

B process: New firmer fixtures; each preheat zone lowered by 10°F; smaller drill-bit sizes for the hole locations displaying unsoldered connections

Three C panels and three B panels were run over the wave solder machine in random order. The defects, in rank order (lowest is best), are shown in Table 13-2.

Table 13-2.   B vs. C processes.

Panels	No. of Defects
B_2	5
B_3	3
B_1	2
C_3	12
C_1	16
C_2	13

The results clearly indicated that the B process was better than the C process, with a 95 percent confidence or 5 percent risk. (It would be tempting to say that the B process, with an average defect rate of 3.3 defects per panel, gave a solder defect rate of $3.3/5.000 \times 10^6 = 660$ ppm. However, with the extremely small sample size of three units, calculating averages of this type would be dangerous.) The stage was now set for a variables search experiment.

DOE Experiment 4: Variables Search

On the basis of the second conclusion in the multi-vari study, the wave solder process parameters in Table 13-3 were selected as the most likely cause of variation and listed in descending order of importance. For each parameter, the "high" (deemed to be the best) and the "low" (likely day-to-day deviation from the best) levels were determined.

Stage 1

Ten panels were run over the wave solder machine set at the high levels of the process parameters and ten panels were

Table 13-3. Design of the variables search experiment.

Code	Process Parameter (Variable)	High Level	Low Level
A	Hot Air Knife Pressure, p.s.i.	14	10
B	Pre-Heat Zone Temperatures	Profile 1	Profile 2
C	Flux Density, gm./c.c.	0.90	0.80
D	Conveyor Speed ft./minute	4	6
E	Conveyor Angle (°)	7	5
F	Solder Temperature (°F)	480	450
G	Solder Dwell Time (sec.)	3.5	3.0
H	Flux Foam Height	1.2	1.0

run at the low levels. The experiment was repeated for two more high levels and two more low levels, run in random order sequence. The results, in terms of the number of defective solder connections, are shown in Table 13-4.

Interpretation

1. All three high levels are better than all three low levels in rank order.
2. High-level median = 4; low-level median = 46; D = $46 - 4 = 42$; $\bar{d} = (9+3)/2 = 6$.

Therefore, the $D{:}\bar{d}$ ratio is 42:6, which is greater than the minimum of 1.25:1. Control limits = median $\pm$ 2.776 $\times$ $\bar{d}/$ 1.81 = median $\pm$ 2.776 $\times$ 6/1.81 = median $\pm$ 9.2. High control limits = 46 $\pm$ 9.2 = 55.2 and 35.8; low control limits = 4 $\pm$ 9.2 = 13.2 and -5.

Conclusion

Stage 1 is successful. The Red X and Pink X variables are among the listed variables. In Stage 2, ten panels were run for each combination shown in the first column of Table 13-5. The suffixes L and H denote the low level and high level of each variable, while R_L and R_H denote the remaining variables all at their low levels and high levels respectively.

Table 13-4. Variables search—Stage 1 (ballpark).

High Level Defects	Low Level Defects
4	42
5	46
2	51

Table 13-5.   Variables search—Stage 2 (elimination of unimportant variables).

Variables Combination	Output	Median	Control Limits	Interpretation
A_LR_H	13	4	−5.2 and 13.2	A not important
A_HR_L	38	46	35.8 and 55.2	
B_LR_H	12	4	−5.2 and 13.2	B not important
B_HR_L	39	46	35.8 and 55.2	
C_LR_H	32	4	−5.2 and 13.2	C important, along
C_HR_L	15	46	35.8 and 55.2	with another variable
D_LR_H	20	4	−5.2 and 13.2	D important, along
D_HR_L	21	46	35.8 and 55.2	with another variable
E_LR_H	25	4	−5.2 and 13.2	E important, along
E_HR_L	22	46	35.8 and 55.2	with another variable
F_LR_H	10	4	−5.2 and 13.2	F not important
F_HR_L	40	46	35.8 and 55.2	
G_LR_H	9	4	−5.2 and 13.2	G not important
G_HR_L	42	46	35.8 and 55.2	
H_LR_H	8	4	−5.2 and 13.2	H not important
H_HR_L	38	46	35.8 and 55.2	

Conclusion

1. Variables *A, B, F, G,* and *H* are unimportant and the interaction effects associated with each are also unimportant.
2. Variables *C, D,* and *E* are important and the interaction effects associated with each are also important and should be quantified.
3. A capping run with *C, D,* and *E* combined is in order (see Table 13-6).

Conclusion

Variables *C, D,* and *E* when combined approximate closely the results of Stage 1. Therefore, these variables and

Table 13-6. Variables search—capping run.

Variables Combined	Output	Median	Control Limits	Interpretation
C_L D_L E_L R_H	43	4	−5.2 and 13.2	Search is finished
C_H D_H E_H R_L	7	46	35.8 and 55.2	

their interaction effects need to be quantified in Stage 4—a factorial analysis (see Tables 13-7 and 13-8). From the factorial analysis, the ANOVA table of Table 13-8 was constructed, according to the rules of a full factorial (2^3) experiment.

Conclusion

The last row of Table 13-8 clearly shows the quantification of the three main variables C, D, and E as well as their interaction effects. The most important variable is a three-factor interaction between C, D, and E; that is, between flux density, conveyor speed, and conveyor angle. Factor C, the flux density, is the second most important variable and factor E, the conveyor angle, is the third most important variable. The two factor interactions can be considered negligible.

For best results, the flux density, conveyor speed, and conveyor angle all had to be kept at their high levels. The capping run indicated that the solder defect rate had been reduced from the original defect rate of 3,111 ppm to 80–140 ppm—an improvement of over 20:1!

DOE Experiment 5: B vs. C Validation

Even though the capping run of the variables search experiment had indicated outstanding success, it was felt that a validation of the optimum levels of the wave solder process should be verified ten days later. The objective was to make sure that there were no uncontrolled variables in the process that could negate the improvement.

Table 13-7. Variables search—Stage 4 (factorial analysis).

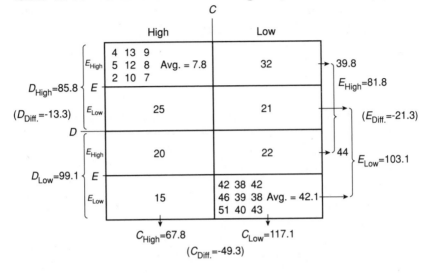

Table 13-8. Variables search—Stage 4 (ANOVA table).

C	D	E	CD	CE	DE	CDE	Output
+	+	+	+	+	+	+	7.8
−	+	+	−	−	+	−	32
+	+	−	+	−	−	−	25
−	+	−	−	+	−	+	21
+	−	+	−	+	−	−	20
−	−	+	+	−	−	+	22
+	−	−	−	−	+	+	15
−	−	−	+	+	+	−	42.1
−49.3	−13.3	−21.3	+8.9	−3.9	+8.9	−53.3	

C process: All process parameters at levels in Experiment 1, except for new firmer fixtures, lower pre-heat zones, and smaller drill-bit sizes for the hole locations in the printed circuit boards

B process: Above *C* process condition, except for flux density at 0.9 gm/c.c., conveyor speed at 4 ft/min, and conveyor angle at 7° incline

Ten panels were run with the C process and ten panels with the B process in random order. The defects, in rank order (lowest is best), are shown in Table 13-9.

Conclusion

The results indicated that the improvements registered in the variables search experiment were now validated, with the new B process better than the old C process, with a 95 percent confidence.

DOE Experiment 6: Optimization Through a Full Factorial

A rigorous approach to optimization required that the two main variables—flux density and conveyor angle—be varied to slightly different levels, using a 2^2 full factorial experiment. Two levels were chosen for flux density—the best level of 0.9 gm/c.c. (from the variables search experiment) and a possibly better level of 0.85 gm/c.c. Similarly, two levels were chosen for conveyor angle—the best level of 7° (from the variables search experiment) and a possibly better level of 6°. Table 13-10 shows the number of defects resulting from the 2^2 full factorial experiment, run with ten panels for each combination, along with replication and randomization.

Table 13-9.   B vs. C processes.

Panels	No. of Defects
B_1	3
B_3	3
B_2	4
C_2	25
C_3	31
C_1	29

Table 13-10. 2² full factorial.

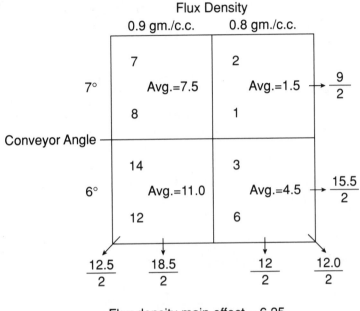

Flux density main effect = 6.25
Conveyor angle main effect = 3.25
Interaction effect = 0.25

Conclusion

The full factorial experiment indicates that the flux density should be reduced to 0.85 gm/c.c. while the conveyor angle should be retained at 7°, the level previously indicated in the variables search experiment. This combination would result in a solder defect level of approximately 30 ppm—an even further reduction of almost 4:1.

DOE Experiment 7: Final Optimization Through Scatter Plots

The variables search experiment indicated that the two most important variables (besides the three-factor interaction) were the flux density and the conveyor angle. The other process parameters were unimportant. The full factorial experiment confirmed that although the flux density could be reduced to give even better results, the conveyor angle seemed to be optimum at 7°.

The purpose of the scatter plot is to determine the very best flux density and its realistic tolerances before solder defects reach unacceptable levels. While other process parameters were kept constant, flux densities were varied from 0.74 to 0.90 gm/c.c. and the ppm levels recorded. The results are shown in Figure 13-2.

The plot in Figure 13-2 shows a sharp increase in the defect levels below flux densities of 0.76 and above 0.84 gm/c.c., especially the latter. If a maximum defect level of 20 ppm is allowed for the wave solder process, the scatter plot indi-

Figure 13-2.   Flux density scatter plot.

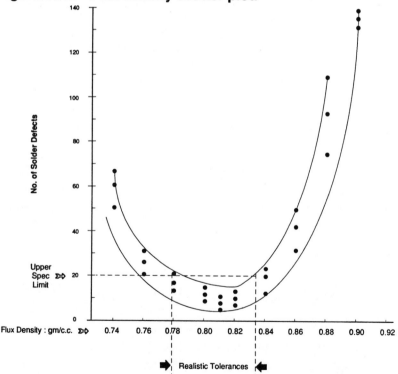

cates that the flux density tolerance can only be between 0.78 and 0.82 gm/c.c. The target value is 0.80 gm/c.c. If precontrol (see Part III) is used to monitor the flux density as a process parameter, its P-C lines should be between 0.79 and 0.81 gm/c.c.

Positrol

The three important variables—flux density, conveyor angle, and conveyor speed—identified in the variables search experiment are controlled with a Positrol plan, as shown in Table 13-11. (See Part III for an explanation of Positrol, process certification, and precontrol.)

These key process parameters were controlled with precontrol.

Process Certification

The quality peripherals associated with the wave solder process were controlled, as shown in Table 13-12.

Table 13-11. Positrol plan.

Key Variable (*What*)	*Who* Controls	*How* Controlled	*Where* Controlled	*When* (How Frequently) Controlled
Flux Density	Solder Technician	Specific Gravity Meter	Flux Container	Once/Hour
Conveyor Angle	Solder Technician	Machine Setting	Conveyor	Once/Day
Conveyor Speed	Solder Technician	Counter	Conveyor	Each Model Change

Table 13-12. Process certification.

Quality Issue	Control Mechanism
Solder Technician	Certification of competency; periodic re-certification
Metrology	Assurance of 5:1 accuracy, precision on all instruments
Instrument Calibration	Per published schedule
Materials	PC boards, solder, flux etc. certified with Cp_k of 2.0 minimum
Environment	Temperature, humidity, electrostatic discharge, etc., controlled according to process sheets
Re-certification	Every six months

Summary

This case study shows how any process can have its defect level reduced to near zero. In this example, the wave solder process was reduced from over 3,000 ppm to 600 ppm; to 100 ppm; to 30 ppm; and down to less than 10 ppm! A systematic road map was followed:

Step 1. Multi-vari study
Step 2. Paired comparisons
Step 3. B vs. C
Step 4. Variables search
Step 5. B vs. C
Step 6. Full factorials
Step 7. Scatter plots
Step 8. Positrol
Step 9. Process certification

This road map is not necessarily a rigid one to follow in all circumstances. In fact, no two chronic problems are exactly alike. The number and sequencing of the DOE tools do vary from problem to problem. Yet the elegance of these Shainin techniques and their combined power can make any chronic problem disappear.

PART III

Statistical Process Control (SPC)

14

Elementary SPC Tools

SPC Tools for Japanese Line Workers

Although the Japanese abandoned SPC tools for the more powerful DOE techniques, there are two exceptions—one minor, the other major. The minor exception is that they sometimes trot out control charts as show-and-tell for visiting American VIPs, so that their advanced DOE methods can escape the scrutiny of fact-finding delegations! The major exception is that they have trained their entire direct labor force in elementary SPC tools, so that they can tackle low-grade quality problems through their quality circles, *Kaizen* (improvement) teams, and employee suggestions.* The result? Instead of having a few professionals to tackle problems, they now have a whole host, albeit low-grade, of problem solvers.

Table 14-1 lists these elementary SPC techniques, often called the seven tools of QC, that every Japanese line worker learns and uses. Because they are both limited in value as well as explained in many texts on the subject of quality

*The number of suggestions turned in by Japanese workers is legendary. Whereas the average number of suggestions per employee per year in the United States is approximately 0.1, the figure in Japan is over 10. In Japanese companies that directly compete with American companies, the number is closer to 50. More important, over 80 percent of these worker suggestions are approved by Japanese management. The quality circles experiment with their own ideas, try pilot runs, and submit their suggestions to management only when they are sure of success. Management approval then becomes almost automatic.

Table 14-1. Elementary SPC tools.

TOOL	OBJECTIVE	METHODOLOGY	WHEN TO USE	TYPICAL USERS
1. PDCA (Plan, Do, Check, Act)	Problem-solve by trial and error	Plan the work; execute; check results; take action if there is a deviation between desired and actual results. Repeat the cycle time till deviation is reduced to zero.	When more powerful tools are unknown	Mostly line workers
2. Data Collection and Analysis	• Assess Quality • Control a Product • Regulate a Process • Accept/reject Product • Interpret Observations	Define specific reason for collecting data, decide on msmt. criteria (attribute vs. variable vs. rank), assure accuracy of measuring equipment (min. 5 times greater than product requirement), randomize, stratify data collection (time, material, machine, operator, type and location of defects), analyze data using several SPC, DOE tools. (Most data are voluminous, gathered haphazardly, unorganized, and of limited use.)	At All Times	Universal
3. Graphs/Charts	• Display Trends • Condense Data • Explain to Others	Select 2 or more parameters to be displayed; determine method of display (bar, line, or circle graphs are the most common); select the most appropriate scales of the parameters for maximum visual impact.	At All Times	Universal
4. • Check Sheets	• Transform raw data into categories	• Determine categories into which data is subdivided (e.g., types of defects, location of defects, days in the week, etc.). Enter quantities in each category.	In preparation for a Histogram or Frequency Distribution	Universal
• Tally Sheets	Groups, Cells in semi-pictorial fashion	• For tally sheets, divide variable being recorded into 10 levels or cells. Plot cell boundaries or mid-points. Make tally (with slash marks) of the number of observations in each cell.		

TOOL	OBJECTIVE	METHODOLOGY	WHEN TO USE	TYPICAL USERS
Histograms/ Frequency Distribution	• Translate data into a picture of the average and spread of a quality characteristic	• Convert tally sheet data into bar graph (histograms) or line graphs (frequency distributions) showing the relationship between various values of a quality characteristic and the number of observations (or percentage of the total) in each value. (A minimum of thirty to fifty observations are required.)	For Process Capability Studies in pre-production or production	Engineers, Technicians, Line workers
5. Pareto's Law	Separate the vital few causes of a problem or effect from the trivial many. Concentrate attention on former.	• Identify as many causes of a problem and the contribution of each to a given effect ($, percentages, etc.), plot causes on X-axis, effects (cumulative) on Y-axis in ascending or descending order of magnitude. Prioritize action on those few causes that account for most of the effect (generally, 20% or less of causes contribute 80% or more of effect)	At All Times	Universal- A fantastic tool for prioritization in Mfg. or white collar work
6. Brain-storming	• Generate as many ideas to solve a problem or improve a process, utilizing synergistic power of a group	• Gather a group most concerned with problem; define problem precisely; ask each member to write down cause of problem or improvement ideas; then, open the floor for an outpouring of ideas, rational or irrational; no criticisms allowed; record ideas; narrow down the most worthwhile ideas.	• Initial Problem- Solving • "Process" Improve- ment	• Quality Circles, • Improvement teams

(continues)

Table 14-1. (Continued.)

• Cause & Effect (Ishikawa; fishbone diagram)	•Organize problem causes into main groups and sub-groups in order to have total visibility of all causes and determine where to start corrective action	• Define the problem; construct a "fishbone" diagram with the major causes (e.g., material, machine, method and man) as the main "branches" and add detailed causes within each main cause as "twigs". Quantify the spec. limits established for each cause where possible, the actual value measured for each cause and its effect upon the problem. If a relationship between cause and effect can be shown quantitatively draw a box around the cause. If the relationship is difficult to quantify, underline the cause. If there is no proof that a cause is related to the effect, do not mark the cause. Prioritize the most important causes with a circle. Experiment with these in PDCA fashion until root cause is located.	Initial attempt at problem solving.	Widely used, especially in Japan, by Quality Circles. Useful only in solving simple problems.
•CEDAC Cause & Effect Diagram with the Addition of Cards	Same as Cause & Effect Diagram & earlier Identification of causes & better worker participation	Workers, at their individual workplaces, identify causes on the spot as they occur. Cards, used to identify such causes can then be readily changed by the workers.	Same as Cause & Effect Diagram	Same as Cause & Effect Diagram
7. Control Charts	Maintain a parameter with minimum variation after major causes have been captured & reduced	DETAILED IN NEXT CHAPTER	• Not for problem-solving. • Production	Engineers, Technicians, Line workers

control, only the objectives and methodology are outlined here. The one exception is the control chart, which will be discussed in some detail in the next chapter. A brief commentary on each of these tools is in order.

1. **PDCA (Plan, Do, Check, Act).** Allegedly taught by Deming, the PDCA cycle has recently been claimed as a Japanese innovation. It is a variant of the traditional problem-solving approach of "observe, think, try, explain." As a problem-solving tool, it has the same poor effectiveness as brainstorming and Kepner-Tregoe detective techniques for solving technical problems.

2. **Data collection and analysis.** This is the first step in the long road to variation identification and reduction. Sound planning is the key to effective data collection. The "why, what, when, where, who, and how" of data must be established a priori, i.e., before the fact. This avoids teams and plants drowning in meaningless and useless data. Common pitfalls include not defining the objective, not knowing what parameter to measure or how to measure it, not having sufficiently accurate equipment for the measurement, not randomizing, and poor stratification of data. Similarly, the analysis of data should be undertaken only with proven DOE approaches rather than with hit-and-miss approaches, such as PDCA, brainstorming, cause and effect diagrams, etc.

3. **Graphs/charts.** These are tools for the organization, summarization, and statistical display of data. As in the case of data collection and analysis, the purpose of using graphs and charts should be clearly established and their usefulness and longevity periodically reexamined.

4. **Checksheets/tally sheets/histograms/frequency distributions.** There are several types of checksheets: for process distribution; for defective items/causes/defect locations (sometimes referred to as "measles charts"); and as memory joggers for inspectors, quality control, and servicers in checking product. Their main function is to simplify data gathering and to arrange data for statistical interpretation and analysis.

Tally sheets are special forms of checksheets to record data, keep score of a process in operation, and divide data into distinct groups to facilitate statistical interpretation.

Histograms and frequency distributions provide a graphical portrayal of variability. Their shape often gives clues about the process measured, such as mixed lots (bimodal distribution), screened lots (truncated distribution), amount of spread relative to specifications, noncentered spread relative to specifications, etc. There are two general characteristics of frequency distributions that can be quantified: central tendency and dispersion. Central tendency is the bunching-up effect of observations of a particular quality characteristic near the center and can be measured by average $(\overline{X})$ of all the observations, mode (the value of a quality characteristic with the largest number of observations), and median (the value that divides the number of observations into two equal parts). Dispersion is the spread of the observations and can be measured by range (R), i.e., the highest observation minus the lowest, and standard deviation, which is approximately one-sixth of range (but only for a normal distribution).

5. **Pareto's Law.** Vilfredo Federico Pareto was a nineteenth-century Italian economist who studied the distribution of income in Italy and concluded that a very limited number of people owned most of its wealth. The study produced the famous Pareto-Lorenz maldistribution law, which states that cause and effect are not linearly related; that a few causes produce most of a given effect; and, more specifically, that 20 percent or less of causes produce 80 percent or more of effects.

Juran, however, is credited with converting Pareto's Law into a versatile, universal industrial tool applicable in diverse areas, such as quality, manufacturing, suppliers, materials, inventory control, cycle time, value engineering, sales and marketing—in fact, in any industrial situation, blue collar or white collar. After the few important causes of any industrial phenomenon are separated from the trivial many, work on the few causes can be prioritized. Figure 14-1 is a typical example of a Pareto chart and its usefulness. Three items, which alone accounted for $2,800 per month of loss (or over

Figure 14-1. Examples of Pareto chart before and after improvement.

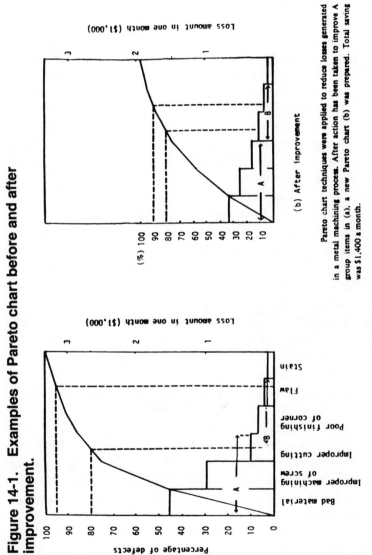

(a) Before Improvement

(b) After Improvement

Pareto chart techniques were applied to reduce losses generated in a metal machining process. After action has been taken to improve A group items in (a), a new Pareto chart (b) was prepared. Total saving was $1,400 a month.

80 percent of the total loss) in (a), were prioritized and reduced to $1,400 per month in (b), before the remaining problems were tackled.

6. **Brainstorming/cause and effect diagrams/ CEDAC.** Brainstorming is a good example of a beautiful technique applied wrongly. In the social sciences, and even in white-collar industrial work, it is a marvelous tool for generating and stimulating the maximum number of ideas, utilizing group synergy. In fact, in value engineering (VE), it is an essential element of the VE job plan. However, its effectiveness in quality problem solving is highly overrated. Even though group ideas are generally better than individual ones, guessing at problems is a kindergarten approach to finding the root cause of variation.

The cause and effect diagram was developed by Dr. Kaoru Ishikawa, one of the foremost authorities on quality control in Japan. As a result, it is often called the Ishikawa diagram or, by reason of its shape, a fishbone diagram. It is probably the most widely used quality control tool for problem solving among blue-collar workers in Japan. However, its effectiveness is poor. At best, it is like playing Russian roulette. At worst, its success probabilities are not much better than the odds in Las Vegas. It is a hit-and-miss process in which finding the solution can take months or even years. Often, because only one cause is varied at a time, interaction effects are missed, which results in partial solutions and marginal improvement in quality. Yet it has a few redeeming features.

Figure 14-2 is an example of a cause and effect diagram, listing all the possible causes that can produce solder defects in a wave solder process. (For the sake of simplicity, only two major branches, machine and machine materials, are shown. For a complete picture, board and electronic component branches should be added to the chart.) Figure 14-2 is an excellent compilation of all the variables that can cause a solder defect. It also highlights with circles those variables judged to be important. In more complex charts, the specification limits and the observed variations from these limits would be recorded for each cause. Such observations, if care-

Figure 14-2.   Cause and effect diagram.

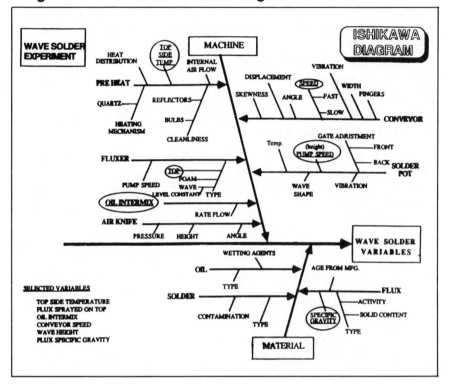

Source: Reproduced, with permission, from a case study by Adi K. Bhote.

fully recorded, can provide some leads in problem solving. In the final analysis, however, guesses, hunches, opinions, and engineering judgment are crude problem-solving tools. Instead, as the great Dorian Shainin suggests, "Talk to the parts; they are smarter than the engineers." What he meant by this is that the parts contain all the information on problem causes and variation, and that their secrets can be unlocked through appropriate statistically designed experiments.

CEDAC is the acronym for "*C*ause and *E*ffect *D*iagram with the *A*ddition of *C*ards." Developed by Ryuji Fukuda, another noted Japanese authority, the technique is explained in detail in his book *Managerial Engineering,* published by Productivity, Inc. (Cambridge, Mass., 1986). CEDAC represents an improvement over the cause and effect diagram, with workers free to change any "branch or twig" cause in the diagram as they observe new phenomena in a process and thereby gain new insights. The use of cards, under the workers' own control, facilitates such instant updating of causes. Worker participation is enhanced, and raw, nonquantifiable information is captured before it "evaporates" in tedious data gathering. Yet CEDAC suffers from the same judgment weaknesses that cause and effect diagrams contain.

7. *Control charts.* The last of the elementary "seven tools of QC" is the control chart. Because of its wide use and misuse, a good portion of the next chapter will be devoted to it.

15

Control Charts vs. Precontrol: Horse and Buggy vs. the Jet Age

In the minds of many, quality professionals and nonprofessionals alike, the control chart is synonymous with statistical process control. For a number of years it held center stage in the discipline that used to be called statistical quality control. The American Society for Quality Control used the chart as its emblem until 1989. Now the logo has been changed to a large Q placed on a grid background. The disappearance of the control chart will be considered by many as a sign of progress.

The Roller Coaster History of Control Charts

Developed by Dr. Walter Shewhart sixty years ago, the control chart quickly became a bridge between the academic world of the laboratory and the hardheaded world of production. In the post–World War II period, however, as walls got plastered with control charts, their usefulness began to be challenged. No tools had been developed to tackle out-of-control conditions—not even simple tools, such as brainstorming and cause and effect diagrams. Once disillusionment set in, the control chart went out of favor.

By the late 1970s, however, the United States' industrial lead had vanished and its invulnerability stood exposed as a myth. The Japanese challenge evoked an intensive search for the key to quality. SPC seemed to be that key. NBC's documentary "If Japan Can, Why Can't We?" became the continental divide between a pre-SPC and SPC era. The control chart was recalled from exile and received a coronation. Its reign continues. It has been a tyrannical reign, with several original equipment manufacturers (OEM) customers, especially Ford, demanding use of the control chart as a passport to doing business with them. They force control charts down the throats of unknowing or unwilling suppliers, and bludgeon into submission those knowledgeable suppliers who dare point out that the control chart emperor wears no clothes! And, as often happens, the royal court is filled with camp followers, hangers-on, and charlatans who exploit the desperation of companies to gain a foothold on the SPC bandwagon by offering courses, tutorials, consultations, and ubiquitous computer software programs, all dealing with the power and glory of control charts. Yet quality progress, as measured by C_p and C_{pk}, has barely inched forward in the majority of American companies, despite the widespread use of control charts. In nontechnical terms, this means that the reduction of variation, an urgent overall quality goal, has hardly made any progress. Sooner or later, as statistical literacy is increased, disillusionment will once again set in and *control charts will become obsolete, as they already are in Japan.*

A Maintenance Tool, at Best

This critique of control charts does not mean that they serve no useful purpose whatsoever. *Their main function, past and present, is to maintain a process under control, once its inherent variation has been reduced through the design of experiments.* The key word here is *maintain.* The most common misuse of control charts is to put them into effect in order to solve a problem. If there is a known problem, the application of control charts will not solve it, but will simply confirm that a problem exists, making control charting redundant. A second misuse is to introduce a control chart without any prior knowledge of whether process capability exists or not. In this case, the control chart may give the answer, but only a day or two later, after 80 to 150 readings have been taken and trial control limits calculated. As we shall see later in this chapter, the technique of precontrol is a simpler and more cost-effective maintenance tool than is a control chart, and it can gauge process capability in one-hundredth the time taken by the latter.

Advantages Over Frequency Distributions

Frequency distributions, although they can translate masses of data into a neat picture and can provide clues about a process, have two limitations. First, they are static because they do not capture variations with time. Second, they cannot distinguish between small, random variations caused by a large number of factors, referred to as unassignable causes, and large, nonrandom variations caused by a small number of assignable factors. A control chart overcomes these obstacles. It adds the important time dimension, so that trends with time can be spotted, and it separates in a vague way the effects of unassignable causes that require no corrective action from the assignable causes that must be investigated and corrected.

The Mechanics of Control Charts for Variables (X̄ and R Charts)

A full treatment of control chart practices could fill an entire book. Because there is a huge volume of published materials—texts, videotapes, and computer programs—on control charts, it is assumed that most readers have some familiarity with them. In this chapter, only a few highlights are examined in order to compare control charts and precontrol.

Table 15-1 is a step-by-step procedure for generating control charts for use with variables data (i.e., where there are scalar measurements that are continually variable, such as dimensions, weights, voltages, temperatures, speeds, etc.).

Table 15-2 lists the formulas for calculating the upper and lower control limits for $\overline{X}$ and R charts, as well as for the most common of the attribute charts, p and c charts. (Attributes, as contrasted with variables, are discrete numbers associated with accept-reject, pass-fail, go/no go criteria). In

Table 15-1. Trial control chart procedure.

1. Select key product parameter(s) from the process to be controlled, based on importance/jeopardy.
2. Take periodic samples (say, every ½ hr., or 1 hr., etc.) from the process with a subgroup size of, say, 4 or 5 units in each sample.
3. Run the process to obtain a minimum of 25 to 30 such samples.
4. For each subgroup, calculate average, $\overline{X}$, and range, R.
5. Calculate grand average, $\overline{\overline{X}}$, of all subgroup averages and calculate average range, $\overline{R}$, of all subgroup ranges.
6. Calculate upper control limit ($UCL_{\overline{X}}$) and lower control limit ($LCL_{\overline{X}}$) for $\overline{X}$ chart:

$$UCL_{\overline{X}} = \overline{\overline{X}} + A_2\overline{R}$$
$$LCL_{\overline{X}} = \overline{\overline{X}} - A_2\overline{R}$$

(See tables for A_2 values of appropriate subgroup sizes)

7. Calculate upper control limit (UCL_R) and lower control limit (LCL_R) for R chart:

$$UCL_R = D_4\overline{R}$$
$$LCL_R = D_3\overline{R}$$

(See tables for D_4 and D_3 values of appropriate subgroup sizes)

8. Plot $\overline{X}$ and R charts. Draw in the control limits for $\overline{X}$ and R. If all $\overline{X}$ and R points (for each subgroup) are within their respective control limits, the process is considered stable—a constant cause system.
9. If one or more $\overline{X}$ or R points fall outside their respective control limits, use statistical problem-solving methods to find assignable causes.

Table 15-2. Control chart formulas.

Chart	Central Line	Lower Control Limit	Upper Control Limit
$\overline{X}$	$\overline{\overline{X}}$	$\overline{\overline{X}} - A_2 \overline{R}$	$\overline{\overline{X}} + A_2 \overline{R}$
R	R	$D_3 \overline{R}$	$D_4 \overline{R}$
% Defective: p	$\overline{p}$	$\overline{p} - 3\sqrt{\dfrac{\overline{p}\,(1\text{-}\overline{p})}{n}}$	$\overline{p} + 3\sqrt{\dfrac{\overline{p}\,(1\text{-}\overline{p})}{n}}$
No. of Defective: c	$\overline{c}$	$\dfrac{\overline{c} - 3\sqrt{\overline{c}}}{n}$	$\dfrac{\overline{c} + 3\sqrt{\overline{c}}}{n}$

PROCESS LIMITS

Upper Process Limit $\overline{\overline{X}} + 3\,\overline{R}/d_2*$
Lower Process Limit $\overline{\overline{X}} - 3\,\overline{R}/d_2$
$*\sigma \text{Population} = \sigma^1 = \overline{R}/d_2$

Subgroup Size n	A_2	D_3	D_4	d_2
4	0.73	0	2.28	2.059
5	0.58	0	2.11	2.326

addition, the table provides important formulas for calculating the upper and lower limits of individual values likely from the process. This is an important step that most control chart practitioners do not even know, much less use.

Theoretical Underpinning for Control Charts

Control chart theory is based upon the central limit theorem in statistics. This states that when subgroups or samples are periodically drawn from a process and the average of each subgroup calculated, these averages will form a normal distribution, regardless of the distribution of the individual readings of the process or parent population. In other words, the individual readings in the process may have a nonnormal, skewed, and even a discontinuous distribution. But subgroup averages drawn from any such process will be normally distributed and the algorithms of the normal distribution can be applied. The most important of these algorithms is as follows: The area under a normal curve bounded by two lines that are three standard deviations on either side of the average is 99.73 percent of the total area in the normal distribution. A shorthand description is that the area within $\overline{X} \pm 3\,\sigma$ of a normal distribution is 99.73 percent, where $\overline{X}$ is the average and σ is the Greek symbol for standard deviation, a measure of spread.

In control charts for $\overline{X}$, when subgroup averages are calculated, the derived upper and lower control limits represent the $\overline{X} \pm 3\,\sigma$ limits of the subgroup averages. Hence, if any subgroup average, $\overline{X}$, falls outside these limits, there is a $1 - 99.73$ percent, i.e., 0.27 percent, probability that this average reading occurred entirely by chance, but a 99.73 percent confidence that it was caused by a nonrandom, assignable cause. The process must be stopped and an investigation begun to correct the problem. On the other hand, even if there is considerable variation among the $\overline{X}$ readings, but they fall within the upper and lower control limits, the variation is due to small, random, unassignable causes that are not worth investigating, and the process should be left alone.

Two Case Studies Highlighting the Weaknesses of Control Charts

Theoretical models, however, do not always neatly fit real-life situations. The several weaknesses of control charts are best illustrated by two case studies.

Control Charting a Bushing Parameter

In a machine shop operation, a bushing had to be made to a length of $0.500'' \pm 0.002''$, a typical requirement. Table 15-3 shows the data of subgroups of five units, drawn from the

ry hour on the hour. From the recorded data, the
, and the range, R, are calculated for each sub-
m the several $\overline{X}$ and R values, the grand average,
average range $\overline{R}$, are derived. The formulas for the
lower control limits shown in Table 15-2 are then
npute these limits for both the $\overline{X}$ and R charts.
sults are drawn in Figure 15-1. It clearly shows
group averages, $\overline{X}$, are within the upper and lower
its in the $\overline{X}$ chart. Similarly, all the subgroups, R,
the upper and lower control limits for the R chart.
tes that the trial control chart, which, incidentally,
nd a half shifts and many readings to complete, has
d that the process is stable (otherwise called a
ause system in statistical parlance). Process capa-
ow assured and full production can go forward,
to fabricate thousands and thousands of units.

1. Bushing length: $\overline{X}$ and R charts.

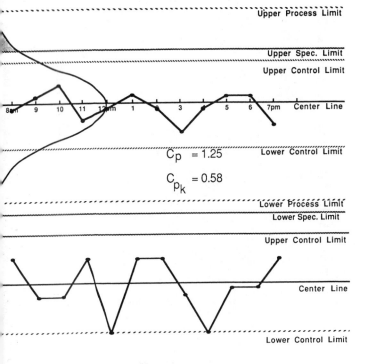

Table 15-3. Typical control chart data.

Bushing Length
Specification .500" ± .002"

Sample #	8 am	9	10	11	12 pm	1	2	3	4	5	6	7 pm
1	.501"	.501"	.502"	.501"	.501"	.500"	.500"	.500"	.501"	.502"	.501"	.500"
2	.501"	.501"	.501"	.502"	.501"	.500"	.501"	.501"	.501"	.502"	.502"	.500"
3	.500"	.501"	.502"	.501"	.501"	.502"	.501"	.501"	.501"	.501"	.501"	.501"
4	.501"	.501"	.501"	.500"	.501"	.502"	.501"	.501"	.501"	.502"	.501"	.502"
5	.502"	.502"	.501"	.500"	.501"	.502"	.500"	.502"	.501"	.501"	.501"	.501"
Sum of "X"s	2.505"	2.506"	2.507"	2.504"	2.505"	2.506"	2.505"	2.503"	2.505"	2.508"	2.506"	2.504"
$\bar{X}_1$	.501"	.5012"	.5014"	.5008"	.5010"	.5012"	.5010"	.5006"	.5010"	.5012"	.5016"	.5008"
R_1	.002"	.001"	.001"	.002	.000"	.002"	.002"	.001"	.000"	.001"	.001"	.002"

process
average,
group. F
$\bar{X}$, and t
upper a
used to

The
that all
control
are with
This ind
took one
establish
constant
bility is
suppose

Figure 1

Yet if specification limits* are drawn, as shown in Figure 15-1, it can be seen that the upper control limit for *averages* is dangerously close to the upper specification limit for *individual readings*. Even without much statistical sophistication, any layperson can reason that if average values are close to a limit, the individual values that make up the average can go beyond that limit. More precisely, the projected spread of individual values can be calculated by the formulas shown in Table 15-2 for process limits.† Figure 15-1 depicts these process limits. The upper process limit is 0.007″ above the upper specification limit, indicating that 5 percent to 7 percent of the bushings are likely to be defective. *So here is a control chart indicating that all is well and that production should continue full speed ahead, when, in actuality, the process is likely to produce a totally unacceptable rate of defective parts!* In quality control literature, this is referred to as a β risk, the risk of accepting product that should be rejected. In this case, the β risk is at least 5 percent.‡

Control Charting a Sensor Capacitance

An electronic element for sensing atmospheric pressure in an automobile has a capacitance requirement in the range of 31 to 45 pico-farads (pf). Figure 15-2 shows $\overline{X}$ and R control charts for the process.

In contrast to the first case study, both the $\overline{X}$ and R charts show several average and range readings outside the upper and lower control limits. The inference is that the process is hopelessly out of control and must be stopped dead in its tracks until corrected. Yet production claimed that it had

---

*Many control chart purists do not allow specification limits to be shown on control charts, because they believe that such a practice inhibits the necessity for continual process improvement, which somehow, almost magically, they believe, can be achieved with control charts!

†Again, in most control chart work, process limits are not even known, much less calculated or used to gauge process capability.

‡If the concept of C_p and C_{pk}, explained in Chapter 3, is used to calculate process capability, this particular process has a poor C_p of 1.25 and a totally unacceptable C_{pk} of 0.58. What a dramatic condemnation of control charts!

Figure 15-2.　Sensor: X̄ and R charts.

Spec: 31 to 45 P.F.

$\bar{\bar{X}}$ = 37.2 P.F. ;　$\bar{R}$ = 2.2 ;　$UCL_{\bar{X}}$ =37.88;　$LCL_{\bar{X}}$ = 36.52;　UCL_R = 3.95; LCL_R = 0

Upper Process Limit = 35.0;　Lower Process Limit = 39.5

C_P = 2.0 ;　K　= 0.04 ;　C_{P_K} = 1.92

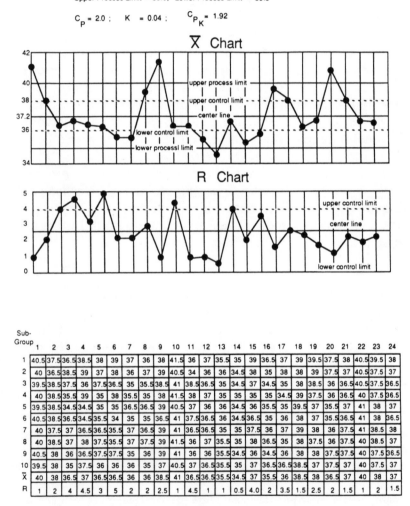

Sub-Group	1	2	3	4	5	6	7	8	9	10	11	12	13	14	15	16	17	18	19	20	21	22	23	24
1	40.5	37.5	36.5	38.5	38	39	37	36	38	41.5	36	37	35.5	35	39	36.5	37	39	39.5	37.5	38	40.5	39.5	38
2	40	36.5	38.5	39	37	38	36	37	39	40.5	34	36	36	34.5	38	35	38	38	39	37.5	37	40.5	37.5	37
3	39.5	38.5	37.5	36	37.5	36.5	35	35.5	38.5	41	38.5	36.5	35	34.5	37	34.5	35	38	38.5	36	36.5	40.5	37.5	36.5
4	40	38.5	35.5	39	35	38	35.5	35	38	41.5	38	37	35	35	35	35	34.5	39	37.5	36	36.5	40	37.5	36.5
5	39.5	38.5	34.5	34.5	35	35	36.5	36.5	39	40.5	37	36	36	34.5	36	35.5	35	39.5	37	35.5	37	41	38	37
6	40.5	38.5	36.5	34.5	35.5	34	35	35	36.5	41	37.5	36.5	36	34.5	36.5	35	36	38	37	35.5	36.5	41	38	36.5
7	40	37.5	37	36.5	36.5	35.5	37	36.5	39	41	36.5	36.5	35	35	37.5	36	37	39	38	36	37.5	41	38.5	38
8	40	38.5	37	38	37.5	35.5	37	37.5	39	41.5	36	37	35.5	35	38	36.5	35	38	37.5	36	37.5	36	38.5	37
9	40.5	38	36	36.5	37.5	37.5	35	36	39	41	36	36	35.5	34.5	36	34.5	36	38	38	37.5	37.5	40	37.5	36.5
10	39.5	38	35	37.5	36	36	36	35	37	40.5	37	36.5	35.5	35	37	36.5	36.5	38.5	37	37.5	37	40	37.5	37
X̄	40	38	36.5	37	36.5	36.5	36	36	38.5	41	36.5	36.5	35.5	34.5	37	35.5	36	38.5	38	36.5	37	40	38	37
R	1	2	4	4.5	3	5	2	2	2.5	1	4.5	1	1	0.5	4.0	2	3.5	1.5	2.5	2	1.5	1	2	1.5

produced thousands of units without a single reject! To some extent, this can be seen from the raw data in the subgroups, where no individual reading is even close to either the upper or lower specification limits of 45 and 31 pf. Further, the projected process limits for individual readings are 39.5 and

35 pf, well within the specification limits. (The projected process spread is slightly narrower than the spread of actual individual readings because the chosen subgroup size of ten was unusually large.)

Here we have the opposite condition from the one shown in the first case study—a control chart declaring that the process should be shut down, when production should in fact continue.* (On a long-term basis, the inherent variation depicted in the process can be reduced, but there is no need to stop production, as indicated by the control chart.) In quality control literature, this condition is called an α risk, i.e., the risk of rejecting a product that should be accepted.

When quality improvements are made (through DOE, not through the mechanism of the control chart), statistics in control chart work automatically make the control limits narrower and narrower, until any little perturbation causes the process to go, artificially, out of control. This flies in the face of all logic. It means that as quality improves, the probability of a stoppage increases! In plain Anglo-Saxon terms, that is nonsense!

The Discovery of Precontrol

Precontrol was developed by the consulting company of Rath and Strong for a major Fortune 500 company that had become disenchanted with cumbersome and ineffective control charts. Precontrol's founder, Frank Satterthwaite, is a brilliant statistician who established its theoretical underpinnings in a comprehensive paper over thirty years ago. Unfortunately, just as precontrol was gaining recognition, the United States, flushed with its economic success in the post–World War II years, threw out all statistical methods in industry, control charts and precontrol included. Then, as SPC became fashionable again in the 1980s and the control

---

*The process capability for this second case is a respectable C_p of 2.0 and a very acceptable C_{pk} of 1.92.

chart became its centerpiece, precontrol started to reappear on the statistical horizon. Three years ago, the ratio of control chart users to precontrol practitioners was 99:1. Today the ratio is 85:15. In a few years, as the simplicity and effectiveness of precontrol is better publicized, the control chart will be relegated to history, as in Japan, and precontrol will become the principal maintenance tool in the SPC world.

The Mechanics of Precontrol in Four Easy Steps

The mechanics of precontrol can be taught to anybody in industry, including line operators, in less than ten minutes! There are four simple rules to follow:

Rule 1: Divide the specification width by 4. The boundaries of the middle half of the specification then become the precontrol (P-C) lines. The area between these precontrol lines is called the green zone. The two areas between each precontrol line and each specification limit are called the yellow zones. The two areas beyond the specification limits are called the red zones.

Rule 2: To determine the adequacy of process capability at that time, take a sample of five consecutive units from the process. If all five fall within the green zone before two consecutive yellow zone results, conclude at the moment that the process is in control. (In fact, with this simple rule, the usual samples of fifty to one hundred units to calculate C_p and C_{pk} are not necessary. By applying the multiplication theorem of probabilities or the binomial distribution, it can be proved that a minimum C_{pk} of 1.33 will automatically result.) Full production can now commence. If even one of the units falls outside the green zone, the process is not in control. To determine and reduce the cause of variation, conduct an investigation. Use engineering judgment (which is not infallible by a long shot) or, better still, multi-vari charts and/or paired comparisons, sometimes followed by variables search or full factorials.

Rule 3: Once production starts, take two consecutive units from the process periodically. The following possibilities can occur:

1. If both units fall in the green zone, continue production.
2. If one unit is in the green zone and the other in one of the yellow zones, the process is still in control. Continue production.
3. If both units fall in the yellow zones, adjust the process setting, if they are both in the same zone. If they are in different zones, stop production and conduct an investigation into the cause of variation.
4. If even one unit falls in the red zone, there is a known reject, and production must be stopped and the reject cause investigated. When the process is stopped, as in 3 and 4, and the cause of variation identified and reduced (or eliminated), Rule 2, i.e., five units in a row in the green zone, must be reapplied before production can resume.

Rule 4: The frequency of sampling of two consecutive units is determined by dividing the average time period between two stoppages (i.e., between two pairs of yellows) by six.* In other words, if there is a stoppage (two yellows), say, at 9 A.M. and the process is corrected and restarted soon after, followed by another stoppage at 12 noon (two yellows again), the period of three hours between these stoppages is divided by six, to give a frequency of sampling of every half hour. If, on the other hand, the period between two stoppages is three days, the frequency of sampling is every half day.

Figure 15-3 is a graphical portrayal of precontrol, with a summary of the four simple rules. (The normal curve on the

*When precontrol was first developed, the time period between two stoppages had to be divided by 24 to determine the frequency of sampling. This was later found to be much too conservative and the number was changed to 6. However, if much greater protection against continuing a process that should be stopped is desired, the frequency of sampling can be increased to 10, 12, 15, even up to 24. In most industrial applications, however, such an increase is not at all necessary.

Figure 15-3. Simple precontrol rules.

Simple Pre-control Rules:

1. Draw 2 Pre-control (P-C) lines in the middle half of Spec. Width.

2. To qualify the process as ready to run (actually determining an instant process capability), 5 units in a row must be within P-C lines (green zone). If not, use diagnostic tools to reduce variation.

3. In production, sample 2 units consecutively and periodically.

Condition	Action
1. 2 units in Green Zone	Continue
2. 1 unit in Green and 1 unit in Yellow	Continue
3. 2 units in same Yellow zone	Adjust
4. 2 units in opposite Yellow zones	Stop*
5. 1 unit in Red	Stop*

*To resume production, 5 units in a row must be within the green zone.

4. Frequency of Sampling. Divide the average time interval between adjacent stoppages by 6.

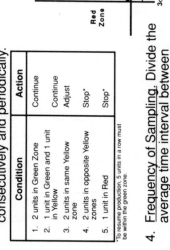
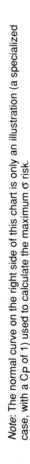

Note: The normal curve on the right side of this chart is only an illustration (a specialized case, with a Cp of 1) used to calculate the maximum σ risk.

right is a special case, where the process width and the specification width are equal. It is used to calculate the maximum α risk and is shown only as an illustration.)

The Statistical Power of Precontrol

The theory behind the effectiveness of precontrol is based on the multiplication theorem of probabilities and the binomial distribution. Although the mathematical derivation of the α and β risks for precontrol is beyond the scope of this book, the following is a summary:

- The worst α risk—the risk of overcorrection, i.e., stopping a process when it should continue—is around 2 percent of the time.
- The worst β risk, the risk of allowing a process to continue when it should be stopped, expressed as product percent defective, is close to 1.5 percent.
- These two risks are "paper" statistical maximums, established from a great number of empirical "in plant" trial and error runs in which we achieved real-world results of virtually zero variations (0.00 percent). Thus, reducing these risks further would make precontrol needlessly less cost-effective.
- When the process width is greater than the specification width, generally C_{pk}s of 0.8 or less, precontrol is so sensitive that it will stop the process at least ninety-nine times out of one hundred and force an improvement investigation.
- When the process width is 75 percent or less of the specification width—C_{pk}s of 1.33 or more—the use of precontrol becomes most productive. The process is in control and precontrol will keep it there.
- When the process width is 50 percent of the specification width—C_{pk} of 2.0—precontrol will allow hundreds and thousands of units to be produced without a single reject.

The beauty of precontrol, therefore, is that it is an ideal incentive/penalty tool. It penalizes poor quality by shutting down the process so often that problem solving with the use of design of experiments becomes imperative. It rewards good quality by sampling more and more infrequently. Control charts, on the other hand, have no sampling rule or built-in flexibility to deal with this important feature.

Charting Precontrol: Easing the Operator's Burden

As opposed to control charts, a graphical record with a chart is not mandatory in precontrol. The machine or process operator has the simplest of rules: "Two greens or one green and one yellow: continue. Two yellows in the same zone: adjust; two yellows in opposite zones or one red: stop." There is no need to distract the operator with long and painful data entries. However, if a precontrol chart is required for historic purposes or as proof of control to a customer or from a supplier, the operator can just make easy slash-mark entries prepared on forms with green, yellow, and red zones. Figure 15-4 is an example of a precontrol chart used to control the thickness of chrome, nickel, and gold deposits on glass in a sputtering machine. The actual readings are recorded for each precontrol sample of two units. From these readings, C_p and C_{pk} values are easily calculated and histograms plotted, if required. There is no need for manual calculations, handheld calculators, or expensive computer programs, an important advantage for small suppliers who do not want or need money thrown at a process with expensive control charts.

Tackling Multiple Quality Characteristics

Precontrol is also a far more economical tool in controlling multiple quality characteristics on a product or process. As an example, if the variations in a thirty-six-cavity mold

Figure 15-4. Typical precontrol chart.

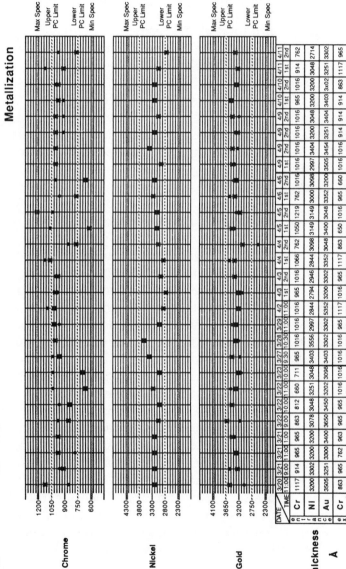

must be monitored in an injection molding machine, the number of readings required to establish even trial control limits in a control chart would average 3,600. By contrast, precontrol would determine process capability with 5 readings for each cavity, or a total of 180 readings.

It is not necessary to monitor all parameters of a product or process continually after initial process capability is confirmed on each parameter. Only the most important or the most troublesome parameters need to be sampled. As an example, in the case of the thirty-six-cavity mold, only the single largest and smallest cavities may need ongoing surveillance. The rest can be monitored infrequently or not at all.

The Versatility of Precontrol

The rule of six samplings between two stoppages need not be associated with time alone. In a very fast operation, where several hundred units are produced in a minute, the quantity of units between two stoppages (two pairs of yellows) can be divided by 6 to determine sampling frequency.

Precontrol is also a versatile technique in determining when to adjust a process or change a tool, rather than a technique tied to fixed or arbitrary time periods. The time to change is when the process drifts into one or the other yellow region. Two yellows give the signal. It is as simple as that.

Another feature of precontrol is its applicability to one-sided specification limits. As an example, consider a product with a minimum requirement of 10 volts, but no maximum. Instead of two precontrol lines drawn in the middle half of the distance between the lower and upper specification limit, there would now be only a single precontrol line. It would be located midway between a desired target or design center and the lower specification limit. A less desirable method would be to locate the single precontrol line midway between the product average and the lower specification limit. In the above example, if the design center were at 15 volts, the single precontrol line would be drawn at 12.5 volts. If the average of the product was 16 and the alternative method used, the single precontrol line would be at 13.

Converting Attributes Into Variables: The "Bo Derek" Scale

Because precontrol deals primarily with the measurement of continuous values, called variables, it may appear to the uninitiated that it cannot be applied to attributes that deal in discrete numbers, such as accept or reject, pass or fail. They may argue that, whereas precontrol is a better substitute for $\overline{X}$ and R control charts, the use of p and c control charts* is unavoidable. Attributes, however, need not be any limitation whatsoever to precontrol.

The trick is to convert an attribute into an "artificial" variable, using a numerical scale from 1 to 10. In what is humorously called the "Bo Derek" scale from the actress's movie *Ten,* the number 10 would correspond to perfection in the quality characteristic being measured and the number 1 would equate with the worst possible reject. There would be other grades of quality ranging between these two extremes. As an example, to convert attributes such as paint, color, scratches, gouges, dents, pinholes, etc., into variables, a committee consisting of the customer, sales, engineering, manufacturing, and quality would grade ten physical samples, ranging from a totally unacceptable 1 to a perfect 10. These physical samples would, then, constitute a "variables scale" to determine the appropriate number for a similar defect in production. In case physical samples are too difficult or too inflexible to develop and maintain, color photographs can be substituted. (It may not be necessary to use a full 1 to 10 scale; a truncated 1 to 5 scale can sometimes suffice.) In a numerical scale of this kind, let us assume that the specifica-

---

*P and c charts suffer from the same fundamental weaknesses as do $\overline{X}$ and R charts, and because they deal with attributes they lack the discriminatory power of variables. They are even worse than $\overline{X}$ and R charts and for this reason they will not be discussed in this chapter.

tion limits are from 4 (worst acceptable) to 10 (perfect). Because this is, in reality, a one-sided specification, a single precontrol line would be drawn at 7.

Weighting Attributes in Terms of Importance

A weakness of p and c control charts is the practice of lumping all types of defects into a single total for attributes. Such charts lack the sensitivity associated with grading defects by importance. In precontrol, every defect mode is assigned a weight in proportion to its importance. This weight, multiplied by the number of defects in that mode, gives the score for each defect type. These scores, when added up, result in a weighted total for a particular time, and a precontrol chart can then be plotted. Such charts have the effect of a magnified scale and are far more sensitive and pinpointed in terms of defect modes than is a catchall p or c chart.

To enable the operator to adjust the production process whenever two consecutive yellow results are encountered, several companies have elected to precontrol each important quality characteristic (defect mode) separately. This procedure pinpoints the need for a particular adjustment.

Figure 15-5 is an example of such a precontrol chart. It expands solder defects, each with its own weight based on the importance of the defect in terms of potential field failure. The precontrol chart highlights the various types of defects found at a particular time, trends with time, and whether or not the weighted defect scores exceed the tight precontrol lines of 50 defects per million connections (i.e., 50 ppm).

A Capsule Comparison of Control Charts vs. Precontrol

Table 15-4 is a comparison of control charts and precontrol. It clearly shows the weaknesses of control charts versus the strengths of precontrol in terms of simplicity, use by

Figure 15-5. A precontrol chart converting attributes into variables on an expanded scale.

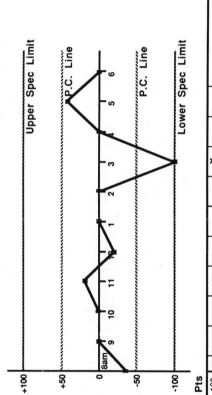

Wave Solder Operation *

Over Solder: Code — Pts

Code	Pts					X	XX		
Solder Short	+20								
Near Short	+10								
Excess Solder	+5								
Capping	+5								
Total									

Under Solder: Code — Pts

Code	Pts			X			
Unsolder Connection	-100						
Insufficient Solder	-20	XX					
De Wet	-20						
Blow Hole	-5			XX			
Total							

comments:

*For attribute precontrol plotting, it is not necessary to have two P-C lines. Because the ideal in attributes is zero defects, a single-sided P-C line is sufficient.

Table 15-4. The advantages of precontrol over control charts.

Characteristic	Control Charts	Precontrol
1. Purpose	• Discover amount of variation caused by "random" and assignable causes	• *Prevent* manufacture of *defects*
2. Simplicity	• *Complex*—calculations of control	• *Simple*—precontrol is middle half of spec. width
3. Use by operators	• *Difficult*—charting mandatory, interpretation unclear	• *Easy*—green and yellow zones, a practical approach for all workers
4. Mathematical complexity	• *Involved*—$\bar{X}$, R, control limits, and process limits must be calculated	• *Elementary*—must only know how to divide by 4
5. Applicability to small production runs	• *Useless for production runs below 500 units*—sampling of 80–150 units before even trial limits can be established	• *Can be used for production runs above 20 units;* precontrol lines predetermined by specs. (which can be narrowed)
6. Recalibration of control limits	• *Frequent*—no such thing in industry as a constant cause system	• *None needed*, unless specs "goal posts" are moved inward
7. Machine adjustments	• *Time-consuming*—any adjustment requires another trial run of 80–150 units.	• *Instant* based on 2 units
8. Frequency of sampling	• *Vague, arbitrary*	• *Simple rule:* 6 samplings between 2 stoppages/ adjustments
9. Discriminating power	• *Weak*—α risk of rejection by chart when there are no rejects is high. β risk of acceptancy by chart (in control), when there are rejects is high. Little relationship to specs.	• *Excellent*—α risk of rejection by precontrol is low; <2% under worst conditions; 0% with Cp_k of 1.66. β risk <1.36% under worst conditions, 0% with Cp_k of 1.66.
10. Attribute charts	P-C charts do not distinguish between defect mode types or importance.	Attribute charts can be converted to precontrol charts by weighting defect modes and an arbitrary rating scale.
11. Economy	*Expensive*—calculations, paperwork, larger samples, more frequent sampling, long trial runs	*Inexpensive*—calculations simple, min. paperwork, small samples, infrequent sampling if quality is good, process capability determined by just 5 units.

operators, mathematical complexity, applicability to small production runs, recalibration of control limits, machine adjustments, frequency of sampling, discriminatory power, conversion of attribute charts, and—most important of all—economy.

The operator can react instantly when two consecutive yellows (still good parts!) are encountered. Precontrol's advantage here makes the attainment of zero defects an actual possibility rather than just a verbal goal.

As a postscript, if precontrol, rather than control charts, had been used in Table 15-3 to control bushing wear, the very first sample at 8 A.M. would have indicated that at least one of the five units checked would have fallen beyond the precontrol lines of 5.001 and 4.999, indicating lack of process capability. This shows the sensitivity of precontrol in stopping a bad process, whereas a control chart would have led one down the garden path all day, declaring the bad process to be good.

Further, if precontrol had been used in Figure 15-2, it would not have shut this process, confirming production's contention of zero rejects among thousands of units.

Among the unconverted who hang onto control charts, Ford is one of the most vociferous and tyrannical. Its quality auditors refuse to accept precontrol because "it is not in the book"! Its professionals, on the surface, appear to be somewhat more logical. They claim that precontrol with fixed specifications, and, therefore, fixed precontrol limits, does not permit continual, never-ending improvement; control charts supposedly produce improvement, with narrower and narrower control limits. However, these professionals miss the point altogether. Ford's argument is tantamount to saying that the temperature in a room can be controlled by a thermometer! Neither control charts nor precontrol are tools for improvement, which can best be achieved through DOE.

Practice Exercise on Precontrol: The Wire Bonder

An automatic wire bonder, which bonds a wire—the thickness of a human hair—to the die and post of a transistor, is put on precontrol to maintain statistical control. The integrity of the wire bond is checked with a destructive pull test on the wire. The specification for the bond strength, before the bond is lifted on either side, is a minimum of 6 gm and a maximum of 14 gm. The initial sample of five units had the following readings: 8.7 gm, 9.0 gm, 9.4 gm, 8.9 gm, 10 gm.

Question 1. What are the values for the precontrol lines?

Question 2. On the basis of the initial sample of five units, is the process in control?

Question 3. How frequently (initially) should a sample of two units be tested for bond strength, assuming that when full production began the period between stoppages (two pairs of yellow) averaged 12 hours?

Question 4. During subsequent production, the results of two sample units, drawn periodically from the process, were as follows. (For the purpose of this exercise, waive the rule requiring five units to fall within the green zone in order to reestablish process capability.)

Sample No.	Unit 1	Unit 2	Action
1	9.4	9.0	_____
2	9.0	8.8	_____
3	8.9	8.6	_____
4	8.5	8.1	_____
5	8.4	8.0	_____
6	8.0	8.0	_____
7	8.0	7.6	_____
8	7.5	7.3	_____
9	13.0	13.0	_____
10	12.0	12.0	_____
11	11.6	11.4	_____
12	11.0	10.8	_____

What action would you take on each sample: Would you continue production or stop?

Question 5. What nonrandom trends do you detect in the data in Question 4? Explain your answer.

Question 6. Assuming that there was no upper specification limit of 14 gm, where would you draw a single precontrol line if the target (or desired) bond strength was at 11.0 gm?

Here are the answers to our six questions:

Question 1. Precontrol lines are at 8 and 12 gm.

Question 2. Process in control. All five units in the initial sample are within the precontrol lines (green zone).

Question 3. Sampling frequency should be 12 hours/6 = 2 hours.

Question 4. Action on sample numbers 1 through 7 and 10 through 12: Continue production. Action on sample numbers 8 and 9: Stop production. (In actual practice, the process must be adjusted or corrected after sample number 8, and then five more units must be drawn and determined to be within the green zone before the sampling of two units is resumed. The same holds for sample number 9.)

Question 5. There are three nonrandom trends in the data associated with Question 4: (1) Bond strengths are getting lower and lower until a correction is made after sample number 8. Probable cause is bond contamination or loss of bond energy. In any case, the trend needs to be investigated, quite apart from whether production continues or stops. (2) The second reading in each sample is almost always lower than the first. The probable cause may be in the measuring instrument or in the fixture. (3) Sample number 9 indicates an overcorrection (pull strengths too high).

Question 6. With the target at 11.0 gm and only a single (lower) specification limit, the precontrol line should be midway between the target of 11.0 gm and the lower specification limit of 6.0 gm, i.e., at 8.5 gm.

16

Positrol, Process Certification, and Operator Certification

Part II of this text has now clearly demonstrated that the systematic way to identify, analyze, and reduce variation is not through SPC tools, such as control charts, but through the design of experiments (DOE). What, then, is the true role of SPC? *It is to maintain that reduced variation, to ensure that it stays reduced at all times.* This is the only correct use of control charts—as a maintenance tool, not as a problem-solving tool. But, as we have seen in Chapter 15, precontrol should be a 100 percent substitute for control charts. There is nothing that control charts can do that precontrol cannot do, and furthermore do less expensively and with greater statistical effectiveness.

However, between the end of DOE and the start of precontrol there are three disciplines that must be put into effect: Positrol, process certification, and operator certification (see Figure 5-1).

Positrol

One of the weaknesses of American industry is that its production engineers and technicians attempt to control a *process* by checking the *product* it produces. That is too late. A parallel, in nautical terms, would be to steer a boat by looking at the wake it produces! A process, like a product, has idiosyncrasies, inherent variables that must be identified and analyzed with DOE tools. Chapters 9 and 10 offered examples of a systematic identification of process variables in a press brake, a wave solder process, and a drilling process. The important process variables were separated from the unimportant ones.

The role of Positrol (a term meaning "positive control") is to ensure that important variables (the "what"), identified and reduced with DOE tools, stay reduced with a "who, how, where, and when" plan and log.

Table 16-1 presents such a Positrol plan. The wave solder case study in Chapter 10 identified four process variables—flux, belt speed, angle of incline, and preheat temperature—as process parameters that needed careful monitoring to ensure a 50:1 reduction in solder defects. The Positrol plan determines *who* should measure these process parameters, *how* they should be measured, *where*—specifically—they should be measured, and *when* (how frequently) they should be measured.

Once such a Positrol plan is prepared, its execution must be recorded in a log maintained at the process. It should be filled out by the designated person (who) and monitored

Table 16-1.   Positrol plan for a wave solder process.

Parameter (What)	Specification	Who	How	Where	When
			Measurement		
A 880 flux	0.864 gm./ cc ± 0.008	Lab. technician	Specific gravity meter	Lab	Once a day
Belt speed	6 ft./min. ± 10%	Process technician	Counter	Board feed	Each model change
Angle of incline	7° ± 20%	Process technician	Angle scale	Tilt post	Each model change
Pre-heat temp.	220°F ± 5°	Automatic	Thermo-couple	Chamber entrance	Continuous

periodically by the supervisor, process engineer, or quality control.

Table 16-2 is an example of a Positrol log on a sputtering machine used to metallize glass, with a layer of chrome, nickel, and gold on one side of the glass, and chrome and gold on the other side. Previous history on the sputtering machine indicated continued "in and out" rejects for metal adhesion on the glass. The process engineer would "twiddle" one knob after the other in an effort to control adhesion, ending up "chasing his own tail" and becoming thoroughly confused as to what to do. DOE experiments identified four factors— power, gas pressure, speed, and vacuum—as important and established the maximum outer limits for each of these parameters with scatter plots. A log was then maintained by the operators four times a day on this three-shift operation. With DOE and Positrol, the rejects were reduced to zero!

In many cases, it is more economical to use precontrol, rather than a log, for process control. Precontrol has the advantage of being able to lengthen the period between checks on each process parameter if the time between corrections (two pairs of consecutive yellows) is comfortably long. In more modern processes, usually microprocessor-based, parameter tolerances can be designed into the process such that Positrol becomes automatic, eliminating the necessity for either a Positrol log or precontrol. However, DOE tools must be used first to separate important process parameters from unimportant ones and to determine the tolerances on each parameter, before microprocessor controls are designed.

Positrol is a simple, commonsense technique to maintain a process under control. Yet, less than 1 percent of U.S. companies use it to monitor processes, even where SPC has been widely used to monitor the products produced by these processes. To paraphrase a Hollywood cliché, "You have a long way to go, baby!"

Process Certification and Murphy's Law

The humorous, but real, foundation of process certification is Murphy's Law, the universal adage that states, "If something *can* go wrong, it *will!*"

Table 16-2. Positrol log.

PROCESS: METALLIZATION MACHINE: 903 WEEK ENDING: 6-20

MACHINE PARAMETERS		MONDAY 6a	12p	6p	12a	TUESDAY 6a	12p	6p	12a	WEDNESDAY 6a	12p	6p	12a	THURSDAY 6a	12p	6p	12a	FRIDAY 6a	12p	6p	12a	SATURDAY 6a	12p	6p	12a
POWER (W) 800-900	Cr	820	800	820	820	820	832	865	820	820	820	820	820	800	882	861	861	861	861	861	861				
47060-4900	N	4848	4830	4779.2	4779	4772	4772	4797	4779	4779	4779	4817.5	4817.5	4765	4772	4817	4770	4855	4855	4819.5	4819				
2300-2400	Au	2400	2400	2400	2400	2370	2370	2370	2510	2370	2370	2370	2370	2370	2370	2370	2340	2340	2340	2340	2340				
1050-1150	Cr	1066	1066	1066	1066	1066	1066	1066	1066	1111	1111	1127.5	1127.5	1127	114	1127	1127	1148	1148	1148	1148				
2300-2400	Au	2400	2400	2400	2400	2370	2370	2370	2570	2370	2370	2570	2570	2370	2570	2370	2340	2340	2340	2340	2340				
GAS PRESSURE (μ) 3.0	Cr	3.0	3.0	3.0	3.0	3.0	3.0	3.0	3.0	3.0	3.0	3.0	3.0	3.0	3.0	3.0	3.0	3.0	3.0	3.0	3.0				
3.0	N	3.0	3.0	3.0	3.0	3.0	3.0	3.0	3.0	3.0	3.0	3.0	3.0	3.0	3.0	3.0	3.0	3.0	3.0	3.0	3.0				
9.5	Au	9.5	9.5	9.5	9.5	9.5	9.5	9.5	9.5	9.5	9.5	9.5	9.5	9.5	9.5	9.5	9.5	9.5	9.5	9.5	9.5				
9.5	Cr	9.5	9.5	9.5	9.5	9.5	9.5	9.5	9.5	9.5	9.5	9.5	9.5	9.5	9.5	9.5	9.5	9.5	9.5	9.5	9.5				
9.5	Au	9.5	9.5	9.5	9.5	9.5	9.5	9.5	9.5	9.5	9.5	9.5	9.5	9.5	9.5	9.5	9.5	9.5	9.5	9.5	9.5				
SPEED (IPM) 4.0	Cr	4.0	4.0	4.0	4.0	4.0	4.0	4.0	4.0	4.0	4.0	4.0	4.0	4.0	4.0	4.0	4.0	4.0	4.0	4.0	4.0				
7.5	N	7.5	7.5	7.5	7.5	7.5	7.5	7.5	7.5	7.5	7.5	7.5	7.5	7.5	7.5	7.5	7.5	7.5	7.5	7.5	7.5				
7.0	Au	7.0	7.0	7.0	7.0	7.0	7.0	7.0	7.0	7.0	7.0	7.0	7.0	7.0	7.0	7.0	7.0	7.0	7.0	7.0	7.0				
5.5	Cr	5.5	5.5	5.5	5.5	5.5	5.5	5.5	5.5	5.5	5.5	5.5	5.5	5.5	5.5	5.5	5.5	5.5	5.5	5.5	5.5				
7.0	Au	7.0	7.0	7.0	7.0	7.0	7.0	7.0	7.0	7.0	7.0	7.0	7.0	7.0	7.0	7.0	7.0	7.0	7.0	7.0	7.0				
VACUUM 3x10^-6		3×10^{-6}	3×10^{-6}	3×10^{-6}	3×10^{-6}	3×10^{-6}	3×10^{-6}	3×10^{-6}	3×10^{-6}	3×10^{-6}	3×10^{-6}	3×10^{-6}	3×10^{-6}	3×10^{-6}	3×10^{-6}	3×10^{-6}	3×10^{-6}	3×10^{-6}	3×10^{-6}	3×10^{-6}	3×10^{-6}				
		3×10^{-6}	3×10^{-6}			3×10^{-6}	3×10^{-6}			3×10^{-6}	3×10^{-6}			3×10^{-6}	3×10^{-6}			3×10^{-6}	3×10^{-6}						
CHECKED BY																									
# OF RUNS AT END OF EACH SHIFT		12		14		10		9		5		9		7		8		9		8					

COMMENTS/PROBLEM CAUSE

The major causes of variation—design, processes, materials—can be reduced with DOE and maintained with SPC. But there are a number of peripheral causes of poor quality, scores of little Murphies lurking around the corner, that can negate and checkmate all these fine preventive measures. The immortal Murphy does not, however, constitute a prefabricated, all-purpose, fully exonerating excuse for shortsighted failures to attack and remove these peripheral causes of poor quality—each of minor importance by itself, but which collectively can spell quality disaster. The quality peripherals can be divided into three broad categories: systems, environment, and supervision. Table 16-3 presents a partial listing of various quality peripherals that must be investigated before a particular process can be certified to produce good quality.

Process certification starts with a checklist of various quality peripherals that must be evaluated. Not all the checkpoints listed in Table 16-3 are applicable in all situations.

Table 16-3. A quality peripherals checklist for process certification.

QUALITY SYSTEM	ENVIRONMENT	SUPERVISION
• EFFECTIVE CONFIGURATION MGMT.	• WATER/AIR PURITY	• CLEAR QUALITY GOALS
• ENGINEERING CHANGE CONTROL	• DUST/CHEMICALS CONTROL	• CLEAR INSTRUCTIONS
• MEASURING SYSTEM: ACCURACY, PRECISION, BIAS*	• TEMP./HUMIDITY CONTROL	• COMBINING TASKS
• EQUIP./INSTRUMENT CALIBRATION	• HUMAN/PRODUCT SAFETY	• NATURAL WORK UNITS
• TOTAL PRODUCTIVE MAINTENANCE (TPM)	• LIGHTING/CLEANLINESS	• CLIENT RELATIONSHIPS
• BUILT-IN EQUIP. DIAGNOSTICS	• ELECTROSTATIC DISCHARGE CONTROL	• "OWNERSHIP" THRU VERTICAL JOB ENRICHMENT
• VISIBLE, AUDIBLE ALARM SIGNALS FOR POOR QUALITY	• STORAGE/INVENTORY CONTROL	• FEEDBACK OF RESULTS
• *POKA-YOKE*—MISTAKE-PROOF SELF CHECK		• ENCOURAGEMENT OF SUGGESTIONS
• NEIGHBOR & SELF-INSPECTION OVER EXTERNAL INSPECTION		• COACH—NOT BOSS
• NO PARTIAL-BUILD POLICY		
• WORKER AUTHORITY TO SHUT DOWN POOR QUALITY LINE		

*A technique, developed by Dorian Shainin, called the isoplot, is the best method to ensure the adequacy of instruments used to measure a product.

(Conversely, there are many quality peripherals unique to individual processes or quality systems that are not listed in it.) The checklist is usually drawn up by a process engineer and verified by a quality control engineer. Finally, a team—consisting typically of the process engineer, development engineer, quality engineer, foreman, etc.—physically examines a process or workstation, and only when all the quality peripheral requirements are in place does the process get a "certification" to start production.

Periodically, the team must reaudit such a workstation or process to make sure that variations from policy and sloppy practices have not crept back to cause potentially poor quality. It is recommended that such a recertification be conducted at least once a year. *If such certifications or recertifications were conducted on processes and workstations in the United States, 80 percent would fail even minimum requirements!* How can we build a superstructure of quality when these basic foundations are weak?

Operator Certification

As described in Chapter 4, operators are frequently blamed for poor quality when the real culprit is management. What quality can a worker be expected to produce when he is hired off the street and then given fifteen minutes of instruction by his supervisor? *Training* is the key word. This includes training, testing, certification, and recertification in ever enlarging circles so that the line worker of today becomes the knowledge worker of tomorrow. In Japan, operator training is an essential ingredient in its quality success story. Table 16-4 outlines the differences in operator training between the United States and Japan. In Japan, the line worker is trained so that, later, he can do the work of the technician; the technician so that he can do the work of the process engineer; the process engineer so that he can reach for the work of the design engineer.

Once DOE has identified and reduced important vari-

Table 16-4.   Operator training: United States vs. Japan.

U.S.	Japan
• Short, spasmodic, unfocused	• Long, continuous, geared to major strategies
• Little testing, certification, or recertification	• Testing and certification prerequisites for job and promotion
• No cross-training	• Cross-training for multiple skills
• Training more in classroom	• Training practical, more on-the-job
• Poor or no implementation of training	• Implementation—the key
• No formal career plan for line workers	• Every worker has a management-by-objectives (MBO) plan, with training as the means of achieving that career plan

ables, Positrol has controlled important process variables, process certification has reined in quality peripherals, and operators have been certified, then and only then can SPC be fully applied to the product, using precontrol as a powerful maintenance tool.

PART IV

The March From Passive Learning to Implementation

17

The Management and Practice of Design of Experiments

Change is difficult for human beings. It is even more difficult for corporations. And it is a monumental task for nations, especially one like the United States, which still seems to be basking in the glow of past success. We seem to resist new ideas. Even when we accept them in principle, we feel that they may not be applicable to a particular company. And if that hurdle is crossed, we may not implement them, preoccupied as we are with fire fighting, bureaucracy, and just plain inertia.

The concepts and practices of DOE/SPC outlined in this book present a special challenge because they require a *double* change—first, a change from traditional quality practices to the halfway house of traditional SPC; and second, a change from traditional SPC to the world of DOE and meaningful SPC.

The CEO as the Instigator of Change

As with many other concepts, the adoption and *implementation* of the techniques described here must start with a

205

company's chief executive officer (CEO). He does not have to be an expert in the use of these techniques. But he must know that they exist. He must appreciate their simplicity, recognize their contribution to profitability and customer satisfaction, and feel their power.

The start could be exposure at a seminar. If these techniques can be understood by line workers, surely they can be grasped by CEOs. Exposure should be translated into a set of quality axioms. These are:

1. High quality = low cost = high profitability = high market share = low absenteeism = low personnel turnover = high motivation.
2. Quality is a principal element of corporate strategy and a superordinate value.
3. In the march to world class quality, DOE is the most potent weapon.
4. Defects can and should be outlawed.
5. The achievement of zero defects is only a milestone on the long road to zero variation.
6. Quality is redefined as the systematic identification, analysis, reduction, and eventual elimination of all variation around a target value, in order to maximize customer satisfaction, reduce cost, and enhance competitiveness in the marketplace.

Axioms, beliefs, and understanding should be translated into the following CEO actions:

1. Seek out a DOE/SPC goal champion from among the ranks of top management, who can become thoroughly immersed in these techniques and then pursue implementation as his sole responsibility because of the vastness of the payoff to the corporation. He then becomes the "process owner," the catalyst for change.

2. Make it mandatory for every technical person in the corporation to go through an intensive course on DOE/SPC techniques. Lead by example, rather than by precept.

3. Establish a management steering committee to monitor progress. The use of workshops, as a follow-up to seminars, is particularly useful. Here teams bring in DOE solutions to chronic problems that have sometimes plagued the company for up to three years. Learning by doing is infinitely superior to learning by listening.

4. Measure progress by the number of DOE projects undertaken. Calculate the dollar benefits to the company from quality improvement, cost reduction, and cycle time reductions. Review one or two projects in detail, as a suitable training ground for the CEO's own expertise.

Role of the Design Engineer in Effecting Change

The design engineer, both for the product and for the process, is the principal "hands-on" instrument for change. It is he who will:

- Hear "the voice of the customer," i.e., determine the customer's needs and expectations.
- Determine a target value associated with each product specification, and design to such target values rather than to broad specification windows.
- Use DOE techniques to greatly reduce variation at the prototype stage and during engineering and production pilot runs. (The design engineer should not use full production or the field as an extension of the laboratory to solve problems.)
- Establish product and process compatibility, not by designing processes as mere afterthoughts to fit frozen product designs but by using a product-process interdisciplinary team approach.
- Translate important product parameters into component specifications using DOE techniques (i.e., specify high C_{pk}s for the truly important component specifications while opening up the tolerances on all other component specifications to reduce costs).

The Supplier's Role in Effecting Change

To a large extent, a positive change in supplier responses to DOE/SPC is the responsibility of the customer company. It must reduce the supplier base and promote a partnership with the supplier, so that the latter can, in effect, become an extension of the customer company. It must educate the supplier's management. It must train the supplier's technical personnel in DOE/SPC. It must help solve the supplier's chronic quality problems through the use of DOE tools.

For his part, the supplier should:

1. See that top management follows the same prescriptions outlined for the customer company's CEO.

2. Have his design engineers follow the same guidelines enumerated for the customer company's design engineers.

3. With encouragement of the customer company, get involved very early in the design of the part he is to produce, so that his ideas and expertise can be utilized in determining part requirements. This is known as early supplier involvement (ESI), a practice that is an absolute requirement of the supplier partnership philosophy.

4. Achieve high C_{pk}s for each of his processes, using DOE tools.

5. Maintain these high C_{pk}s with the use of Positrol, process certification, and precontrol and submit precontrol charts to the customer company as proof of excellent quality.

Production Management's Role in Change

As with the CEO, the change in production management must start with a set of production quality axioms. These are:

- The line worker will perform as a highly motivated individual, unless "ground down" by poor management

with a bossy attitude or forced to work in an atmosphere of fear.
- The line worker's brain is as fertile as management's, given training, encouragement, and support.
- Inspection and test add no value to a product and should be drastically reduced.

To successfully implement DOE/SPC, production management must:

1. Drastically reduce fire-fighting quality problems in production by insisting that every important quality characteristic on every new product entering production (at the pilot run stage) be measured for process capability—a minimum C_{pk} of 2.0. (This can be quickly ascertained in an approximate manner by the precontrol rule of five units in a row falling within the green zone.)

2. Establish Positrol, process certification, and operator certification as ironclad disciplines.

3. Maintain reduced variation with precontrol, not control charts.

4. Encourage the concept of the next operation as customer (NOAC).

5. Measure progress:

- *The cost of poor quality: external failure and internal failure and appraisal.* Strive for these costs to be well under one percent of sales.
- *Yields: defects per unit (DPU).* Add up all defects at all workstations and divide by the number of units shipped. Strive for a maximum of 0.01 DPU.
- *Cycle time.* Measure clock time for one unit to go through the plant from one end to another. Strive for a maximum cycle time of no more than twice direct labor time. (This is called theoretical cycle time.)

Quality Management's Role in Change

Many current quality practices are obsolete, requiring as large a metamorphosis in the role of the quality professional as in that of the CEO or production management. He must:

- Become an absolute expert in DOE if he is to be of real value to his company
- Change from being a "policeman" to a teacher, consultant, and coach
- Assist the goal champion in prioritizing areas to attack and problems to solve, and cooperate in interpreting results and measuring progress

The March to World Class Quality

None of the DOE/SPC techniques described in this book are rooted in a *national* culture. It is only an industrial culture that needs to be changed. Can U.S. management effect that change? It is not easy for the mightiest nation on earth, which has taught the principles of quality to the rest of the world, to admit that it too must now learn. But the greatness of the United States is that it is always willing to hold up a mirror to itself, to engage in self-criticism, to analyze, and to improve. In the past, the nation has often shown an amazing resiliency and single-minded purpose in moments of crisis. With that upbeat, can-do, buoyant spirit, we shall *overcome!*

Appendix

An Excerpt From "Better Than Taguchi Orthogonal Tables" by

Dorian Shainin and Peter Shainin

Fractional Factorials

Start with a full factorial, two-level, three variable statistically designed experiment (SDE). The array table for the two levels, $+$ and $-$, would be as given in Table A-1. This 2^3 U.S., U.K. *orthogonal array* has three inputs, factors A, B, and C, providing the signs for the interaction columns by multiplication of the signs.

When the lowercase letter is present for a given cell, the corresponding *single* capital letter input is at the $+$ level; when it is absent, that input is at the $-$ level. For (1), A, B, and C are all $-$. That notation makes it easy, particularly for larger arrays, to apply the Yates' algorithm to estimate the separate independent magnitudes of the influence of each interaction and of each main effect. The # symbol represents

From *Quality and Reliability Engineering International,* Vol. 4 (1988), 143–149. Reproduced with permission from the authors and John Wiley & Sons, Ltd.

Table A-1. Orthogonal array table.

Factor Column Cell No.		A 1	B 2	AB 3	C 4	AC 5	BC 6	ABC 7	$\bar{\bar{y}}$
1	(1)	−	−	+	−	+	+	−	#
2	a	+	−	−	−	−	+	+	#
3	b	−	+	−	−	+	−	+	#
4	ab	+	+	+	−	−	−	−	#
5	c	−	−	+	+	−	−	+	#
6	ac	+	−	−	+	+	−	−	#
7	bc	−	+	−	+	−	+	−	#
8	abc	+	+	+	+	+	+	+	#

the numerical average of the two or more replication results
in each test combination cell.

A four-factor, two-level, full factorial test plan would have
16 cells, and the corresponding table would have 15 columns.
Each of the 15 permits the calculation of a "contrast" between
the $\bar{y}$ (average of the averages) of the $+s$ and the $\bar{\bar{y}}$ of the $-s$,
representing an estimate of the magnitude of the influence
upon y of that interaction or that main effect. One could use
eight cells with four factors, resulting in "a half replicate"
fractional factorial design. In the eight-cell table, one would
plan the fourth factor D to use the signs of any one of the four
interaction columns. Say the experimenter elects to use the
ABC column. Now that contrast column has two names. If its
influence comes out strong, one will not know from such
"planned confounding" whether it was caused by the D main
effect or by its alias, the ABC interaction. Unfortunately, if
its influence comes out not to be significant, that could be the
result of both having an important, not necessarily equal,
influence but in opposite directions, reducing the net effect.
No one would know.

A further "price" paid comes from the fact that with these
four factors, 15 independent influences have to be accounted
for. Consider two axioms of what might be considered the
algebra of $\pm$ signs: (1) Either sign squared $= +$; (2) + times
either sign does not change that sign. Accordingly, since the

sign of D was made equal to the sign of the ABC interaction, one could write, in sign algebra, $D = ABC$; now multiply both sides by BC: $BCD = A$, since B squared and C squared will always be $+$ and thus not change the sign of A. Check it out. Put D in column 7, the alias of ABC. Now multiply the signs of columns 2, 4, and 7. In each cell you will get the sign of A. So the alias of A is the BCD interaction. Notice that one can move letters from one side of the sign equation to the other. No division as in the algebra of Euclidean space. Hence by putting D in column 7, one automatically creates seven aliases:

$A = BCD, B = ACD, C = ABD, D = ABC, AB = CD, AC = BD, AD = BC$

and all the troubles described above for $D = ABC$ unfortunately apply to the other six aliases. But two names for each of seven columns account for only 14 contrasts. The 15th is the $ABCD$ four-factor interaction. Since $D = ABC$, $ABCD$ will always be $+$ for all of the eight cells. The contrast between the $+$ average and the $-$ average has disappeared. All evidence of its influence is lost!

Some Western statisticians have used five factors with eight test cells, a quarter replicate fractional factorial. Now each of the seven columns has four names, and three interactions have no contrast.

Taguchi Orthogonal Array Example

This case history is often used to introduce the Taguchi arrays (see Table A-2).

This actual example of a tile manufacturing experiment was performed by Ina-Seito Co., in 1953. The letters A to G represent seven factors, different raw material amounts and ingredients tested at two levels, 1 and 2 shown in each column. In order to see the equivalence of this array to the previous Western, unconfounded full factorial, substitute $+$ for each level 1, and $-$ for level 2. You will then see how Taguchi inverted columns and rearranged the column positions.

Table A-2. Taguchi orthogonal array table.

Factor Column Test No.	A 1	B 2	C 3	D 4	E 5	F 6	G 7	No. of defectives in 100 tiles
1	1	1	1	1	1	1	1	16
2	1	1	1	2	2	2	2	17
3	1	2	2	1	1	2	2	12
4	1	2	2	2	2	1	1	6
5	2	1	2	1	2	1	2	6
6	2	1	2	2	1	2	1	68
7	2	2	1	1	2	2	1	42
8	2	2	1	2	1	1	2	26

Pros

(a) Taguchi's tables retain the balance, or symmetry feature, of the Western SDEs. When the average of the 1s is compared with the average of another level, 2s or 3s, all the other contrasts have contributed the same combination of their levels to the single level of the factor being evaluated, thus becoming neutralized.

(b) The test work environment in this example was "actual large scale manufacturing," rather than the laboratory. The presence of more variables, including unsuspected ones, permits the data (when replicated) to show more scatter. That would warn the experimenter that he would be neglecting at least one strong variable in the real world of the shop.

(c) When a single strong variable is suspected, these balanced arrays could confirm it as an influential main effect. Examples would be the change of state of a material with temperature, or with pressure; the strength of an adhesive with curing time, or with temperature.

(d) The Taguchi examples claim that one additional actual test set under the best conditions indicated by the earlier experiment confirms conclusions. Sounds good. But unfortunately a confidence interval checks that conclusion; and a higher confidence number provides a larger interval!

Cons

(a) This example depicts a saturated fractional factorial, quite representative of many Taguchi applications. Each of the seven columns has 16 names, 15 interaction causes of variation in addition to the main effect used as a title. Information about 15 additional interactions has been lost. None of this potentially positive knowledge disappears when one uses the constructive alternative, variable search patterns.

Taguchi states (not so clearly?):

> One often hears that ever since experiments by orthogonal arrays have been performed, it has become possible to apply the results of small-scale experiments from the laboratory directly onsite. This is because a factorial effect that is consistent even when the conditions of other factors change has a good chance of being reproduced even if the single condition of scale changes.
>
> However, this *does not guarantee that the experiment will succeed* with the use of the orthogonal array. If there is additivity to the main effects, either an experiment by an orthogonal array or an experiment by changing one factor each time will work well, but if the interactions are great neither will go well. That a certain factor influences the performance characteristic means that this factor imparts effect to the performance characteristic, or in other words that *it performs work*. Therefore, fundamentally, there should be additivity to the quantities of work. But for various reasons, additivity fails, that is interactions exist. *In nearly all cases, interactions is* (sic) *not considered in this book. This is not because there is no interaction. It is because, since there can be an interaction, we perform experiments only on the main effects, having cancelled interactions.* If the interactions are great, no assignment works well except experiments on a certain specific combination. Good results are obtained neither by an experiment on one factor at a time nor by an experiment using an orthogonal array if interactions have been omitted.*

*Genichi Taguchi, *System of Experimental Design* (White Plains, N.Y.: UNIPUB, 1987), p. 171.

We have heard it expressed that all interactions disappear if the variables are plotted on logarithmic scales, or if the output is plotted against an abscissa of the product of the input variables. Having worked with Pratt & Whitney Aircraft for several years in the development of the RL–10 (cryogenic liquid hydrogen–oxygen second stage rocket engine used in Centaur and Saturn), we wonder what the U.S. Air Force reaction would be to: "we could remove the synergistic creation of that engine's power, the hydrogen–oxygen interaction, by changing the scale on which we plot the data"!

(b) Conducting the test sequence in systematic, rather than random, order permits spurious associations. Simply eyeballing these test results clearly shows something other than the seven factors selected is controlling the number of defectives: with time, going from test no. 1 to no. 8, the 16, 17 level descended to 6, then jumped to 68 to start the next cycle down. If factor A were the strong one, as the Taguchi report claimed, that Red X would not have permitted the second 6 to occur with A at level 2!

(c) Not replicating, or repeating, the test results in random sequence prevents obtaining a valid statistical estimate of error or noise. In this example the authors applied the "Shainin test": Use random numbers in place of the reported test data, to check the discriminating ability of any promoted new plan. Taguchi reported from his (very questionable) statistical analysis of his numbers:

16, 17, 12, 06, 06, 68, 42, and 26

that factors $A, D, E, F,$ and G were significant at a risk level of 0.01.

The authors used eight pairs of random numbers, 68 and under, three times. They came out:

60, 32, 03, 11, 04, 61, 66, and 08
61, 24, 12, 26, 65, 14, 54, and 66
01, 16, 60, 36, 59, 46, 53, and 42

and with exactly the same Taguchi statistical analysis:

   (i) the first set showed that factors B, C, F, and G were significant at a risk level of 0.01, with factor A at 0.05.

  (ii) the second set showed that factors A, C, D, and F were significant at a risk level of 0.01.

 (iii) the third set showed that factors A, B, C, and G were significant at a risk level of 0.01, with factor F at 0.05.

Conclusion

The Taguchi publicity has created an awareness in many unsophisticated firms of SDEs. His orthogonal arrays bring the advantage of SDE balance to such firms who may want to show that single, main effect factors they suspect as having a strong influence can be confirmed or denied, provided that they randomize, replicate, and do *not* use the flawed statistical analysis of their results. A professional industrial statistician can keep such a firm from costly, incorrect conclusions, provided that they do *not* recommend the use of fractional factorial designs!

Only 16 tests in a properly conducted full factorial test plan for two, three, or four variables would be necessary to avoid spurious conclusions. Otherwise unsuspected, but often real Red X interactions will still be a problem. *The "fix" looking like a main effect will not stay a fix in later production.* The alternative variable search pattern strategy, *preceded* by objective clue-generating methods such as multi-vari charting, can substantially improve the cost-effectiveness of discovering root cause, controlling variables, including interactions, through using five or more candidate factors together. A sequential, not random, sequence of interchanging levels is employed. Yet replications occur, at Stage I, and later when a swapping of levels stays in control, and from all capping run trials.

Authors' Biographies

Dorian and Peter Shainin have advised and trained personnel at more than 750 companies throughout the Americas and Europe. The Shainins' original strategies, called Statistical Engineering, were primarily developed by Dorian beginning with Lot Plot in 1943. Dorian is a graduate of MIT and began his career as an engineer at United Aircraft Corporation (now United Technologies) in East Hartford, Connecticut. He joined Rath & Strong, a management consulting firm in Lexington, Massachusetts, in 1952, retiring as Vice President of Statistical Engineering and establishing his own consulting practice in 1975. The American Society for Quality Control has certified him as a Quality and Reliability Engineer. The Institute of Management Consultants has designated him a Certified Management Consultant. He was elected Academician by the International Academy of Quality. The American Arbitration Association has appointed him to its panel of Arbitrators. And he has been elected Fellow of the American Association for the Advancement of Science.

Dorian's development and application of original quality/reliability control methods have won him numerous awards from the American Society for Quality Control (ASQC), including its Brumbaugh Award, Edwards Medal, Eugene L. Grant Award and—most coveted of all—the Shewhart Medal, the top honor of the ASQC.

Peter is a graduate of Stevens Institute of Technology (1966) and has been a licensed Professional Engineer (mechanical) since 1970. He began his professional career in the Experimental Test Department of Pratt & Whitney Aircraft in East Hartford, Connecticut. He has had design, foreign licensee coordination, and marketing responsibilities at Marine Construction and Design, a Seattle marine machinery manufacturer, and Skagit Corporation, a division of Bendix. He was chief executive officer of an industrial design and construction firm in Seattle, Washington, before joining Dorian in 1985.

Since joining Dorian, Peter has successfully applied Statistical Engineering to auto parts, paper, laundry products, semiconductor manufacturing, iron and aluminium foundries.

Their current expertise is centered on manufacturing quality control, product reliability, and research and development, for which they provide consultancy services, which are orientated towards exploiting creative and analytical approaches to problem solving.

Index